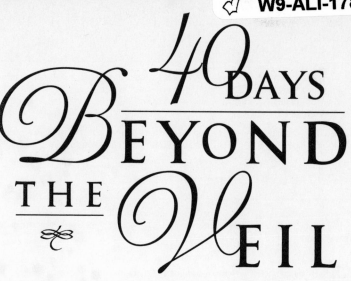

40 DAYS BEYOND THE VEIL

DEVOTIONAL

ALICE SMITH

Regal

From Gospel Light
Ventura, California, U.S.A.

PUBLISHED BY REGAL BOOKS
FROM GOSPEL LIGHT
VENTURA, CALIFORNIA, U.S.A.
PRINTED IN THE U.S.A.

Regal Books is a ministry of Gospel Light, an evangelical Christian publisher dedicated to serving the local church. We believe God's vision for Gospel Light is to provide church leaders with biblical, user-friendly materials that will help them evangelize, disciple and minister to children, youth and families.

It is our prayer that this Regal book will help you discover biblical truth for your own life and help you meet the needs of others. May God richly bless you.

For a free catalog of resources from Regal Books/Gospel Light, please call your Christian supplier or contact us at 1-800-4-GOSPEL or www.regalbooks.com.

Cover design by Robert Williams
Interior design by Steve Hahn
Edited by Deena Davis

Library of Congress Cataloging-in-Publication Data
Smith, Alice, 1950–
    40 days beyond the veil / Alice Smith.
        p. cm.
Includes bibliographical references.
    ISBN 0-8307-3289-6
    1. Meditations. I. Title: Forty days beyond the veil. II. Title.
    BV4832.2.S537 2003
    242—dc22

                                                                    2003014990

1 2 3 4 5 6 7 8 9 10 11 12 13 14 15 / 09 08 07 06 05 04 03

Rights for publishing this book in other languages are contracted by Gospel Light Worldwide, the international nonprofit ministry of Gospel Light. Gospel Light Worldwide also provides publishing and technical assistance to international publishers dedicated to producing Sunday School and Vacation Bible School curricula and books in the languages of the world. For additional information, visit www.gospellightworldwide.org; write to Gospel Light Worldwide, P.O. Box 3875, Ventura, CA 93006; or send an e-mail to info@gospellightworldwide.org.

Dedication

This book is dedicated to my oldest son, Robert, a godly worship leader, husband and father, who has a passionate heart for the Lord.

Contents

The Destination

The Direction

The Delight

The Devotion

The Development

Preface

$\mathscr{I}$ learned early in life that we have time for only one passion. I have chosen Jesus Christ and His kingdom. I love Jesus! He is my *passion!* As short as life is, you, too, have time for only one passion. If you choose the cares of this world, then it's possible that you will miss reaching your Kingdom potential. However, if your passion is Jesus, then your life will be filled with joy, peace and a deep assurance that the lasting relationship you have developed in prayer with God will last for eternity.

This decision to pursue the Lord isn't an easy one. An intimate relationship with God has to be developed. I'm speaking not of rituals or formulas but of friendship. I remember that when I was a teenager, each night I would kneel by my bed to ask God if He would share His burdens with me. Remarkably, over time and by staying faithful to my prayer commitment, the Father began to reveal His ways. My book *Beyond the Veil* was the result of sharing these truths.

The book you now hold in your hands is from a new season in my life. This book contains nuggets of gold the Lord has given to me in my prayer closet during the past five years. Each devotional has a unique and separate truth. I pray that these truths will refashion, remold and renew your spiritual life. I have given you the framework by which you can go beyond the veil and delve deeper into understanding God's ways for your future.

One way that you can experience the full blessing of this book is to combine the reading with a full or partial fast (I have provided information on fasting in the appendix). For example, if you are a morning person, have your quiet time, read one of the devotionals and fast through breakfast and lunch. Be flexible about this, however. You are cultivating a relationship, not performing in a competition. The Lord longs for you to know Him in spirit and in truth. I believe His mercy drops of revelation will teach you how He uses adversity, trouble and, yes, even blessings to develop your intimacy with Him. Come closer to Jesus and go beyond the veil.

I would like to thank and acknowledge:

My husband, Eddie, who has read and reread the devotionals to help me present a clear truth. He has encouraged me and stood with me for over three decades. I love you, Eddie.

Ashlee, my youngest daughter, who has encouraged me to step up to the challenges a woman faces in the ministry. Thank you, sweetheart.

Debbie Walker and *Eraina Lothringer,* who have stood with me for many years. You are true friends, and I love you both.

Thank you, *Deena,* for all the editing, support and encouragement while writing this book. You are a treasure to the Lord Jesus as you tenderly took the inadequacies of my writing skills and fashioned them into a beautiful portrait. You are special to me.

I am truly grateful to my *ladies intercessory prayer group.* These ladies are fearless in spiritual battles as they faithfully fight the good fight of faith. These unique and tenacious women love to pray, and they love to win the victory! I love you, ladies.

To *my heavenly Bridegroom, Jesus Christ:* You are the apple of my eye, the darling of my heart, all that I want or will ever want. Jesus, You are my best friend—it is a pleasure to be your Bride.

Alice Smith

THE DESTINATION

*Every day we have an opportunity to know the Father in a
deeper way than we did the day before, if we will only choose
the path of intimacy with Him. He is our daily destination.
Can you grasp this truth? The journey of intimacy beyond
the veil, into the Holy of Holies, will take you to the place of
abiding in the presence of God, where you will make divine
discoveries about Him and about yourself. Take the journey
with me and I promise you will be forever changed.*

Providence

Therefore do not cast away your confidence,
which has great reward.

HEBREWS 10:35

As I boarded the airplane that evening, I was really weary. The weekend of ministry had been extra hard for some reason, and I felt a head cold coming on. I dropped into the seat for the ride home and dozed off almost immediately. Somewhere in my subconscious, I was still aware of the plane takeoff and the smooth sailing in the sky. The flight attendants had already served everyone, and now the overhead lights were off.

I must have been asleep for most of the trip when the jolt of the plane woke me. The turbulence was some of the worst I had ever experienced. My window seat allowed me to look outside, but there was no visibility, only thick, dark clouds. It was quite unsettling as the plane lurched up and down and from side to side. I strained to see the ground but to no avail.

It seemed like an eternity before the captain came on the intercom. His deep, soothing voice was comforting. "This is your captain speaking. Folks, there is no reason to worry; the haze is thick and the turbulence is rather bad, but ground control has us on their radar and they will help us make a safe landing. We will be landing soon."

Although the plane continued to rock, and it wasn't a comfortable experience, the control room below could see the big picture. They could land the plane safely. At that moment the Lord reminded me that even though at times the circumstances of our lives become tumultuous and hinder our visibility, the heavenly Father always sees the big picture. Not to worry, He has us on His radar screen. We often strain to see in the natural something that God is doing only in the spiritual.

Experiences like this have taught me several things. First, the relationship we maintain with the Father and the atmosphere produced by that relationship are very important. Religious rules and regulations won't carry us when the going gets rough. We need an intimate fellowship with God. Our relationship is found in a deep, abiding faith as we rest in the arms of a good and faithful Father.

Second, if we expect to be prepared to face life's trials, we must maintain a meaningful relationship with the Father. When the bottom drops out and we are rocked by trauma, there isn't time to build a trusting relationship with God. At those times we need to rest in the relationship we've already developed with Him.

Life can be exceedingly challenging at times. Yet prayer should be our first response to a challenge. In answer to our desperate cry for help during life's twists and turns, the Lord is drawing us to listen to His voice. This isn't a step into the dark; it is a step into the light of faith in Him.

This walk of faith insists that we silence our busy and fretful hearts, preparing us to hear God's voice. Our hearing and obeying Him is confirmation that the new nature of Christ is at work in us. Now we just need to step out and trust Him. To the degree that we learn the voice of our heavenly Father and desire to understand His ways, to that same degree we will also hear His voice and walk in His ways. Our personality, intelligence or talents have little to do with it.

The next time you find yourself in the haze of life's turbulence and there is no clear view, draw close to the heart of God. There you will find peace. He has you on His radar screen, and you can trust Him to bring you safely home.

Into the Deep

*He made known His ways to Moses, His acts
to the children of Israel.*

PSALM 103:7

One day, as I sought the Lord in my prayer time, I wept over several painful experiences in my past. "Lord, how can I understand your ways?" I asked. As I waited expectantly on the floor of my prayer closet, the Lord reminded me that His ways are not like our ways, nor His thoughts like our thoughts (see Isa. 55:8). Then He gave me a vision to help me understand the way He works in our lives.

Imagine that you are a leaf that has fallen from a tree. The wind picks you up and blows you into a briskly flowing river—your life. You tumble through the rush of life's demands at an alarming pace. Week after week you bump up against the world system. Although you dip into deeper waters for an hour or two on Sunday morning, seeking a touch of God, the river is unrelenting. On Monday morning you once again get caught up in the twigs and debris of the material world. You know the Lord, and you long to know Him more; yet you are soulishly directed. Instead of depending on the Holy Spirit as your rudder, you aimlessly drift through life—always in a hurry and never quite sure why.

At times you get sidetracked in a tributary. Here the water is still and stagnant, and you get stuck in the mud. The dark night of the soul begins to fall and you suppose that God has forgotten you. Eventually the rains return and the torrents dislodge you from the mire. Back into the river you go, bumping against the riverbank—tumbling and tossing through life. Eventually the river empties into the vast ocean. Get ready! Your life is about to be changed forever. For it is in the depths that God reveals His ways to you. King David said it well: "Deep calls unto deep at the noise of Your waterfalls; all Your waves and billows have gone over me" (Ps. 42:7).

As you earnestly seek the Lord, a large wave crests above you. You cry out to God to know Him, and the wave crashes and washes you with His love. Yet the pull of the current is strong along the ocean floor. As a 12-year-old, I once was caught in an undertow at the beach. To submit to the current would have proven deadly; instead, I resisted and lived. Yet God's ways work differently. He *is* pulling you into the deep in order to bring you to death to self. Do not resist His work.

As the waves continue to break, you are pulled to the ocean's floor where you are helpless. Self-sufficiency is gone and death to self begins. The ocean floor is dark and undisturbed. The only hope you have is divine illumination—God-directed living. From the darkness, the Lord is able to reveal His light on the situation. The pressure at this depth is great. After all, you are now under the weight of almighty God, who wants you to be still and know that He is God. He wants you to resign yourself and to submit to the process. This is no time to fight, struggle or strive with God. For it is here that you learn His ways, which are utterly different from yours.

This process may take months or even years. Death to self creates desperation, and desperation creates a hunger. Hunger provokes a pursuit of God. It is in this pursuit of God that you are led to purity of character and a purging of your behavior.

I have great news for you! What we try to crucify on our own rots, but what the Lord puts to death He resurrects! It is well worth the journey to move from the busy river into the deep waters with God. From this experience you can expect to gain a renewed confidence in the Lord and a huge impartation of faith—not just any faith but *God faith*. This faith is instilled by the Spirit of the Lord and cannot be self-generated. Others cannot go with you into the deep; you must experience it alone.

Do you trust the Father with your life? Are you willing to journey into the deep with God? Don't wait until you understand the process, because you never fully will. It is beyond the mind's ability to comprehend. Just be willing to say, "I'm ready; let's go." Do you want to know God's ways? Then launch into the deep with Him today.

Trust

Those who trust in the LORD are like Mount Zion, which cannot be shaken but endures forever.

PSALM 125:1, *NIV*

When Bryan, our youngest son, was just a small boy, he asked his dad to put him on top of a large seven-foot-high concrete platform at the library. Eddie did so. After a few minutes, Eddie reached out his hands and said, "Jump, Bryan! Daddy will catch you."

Bryan was not so sure. Eddie said again, "Jump, son. I won't let you fall. You can trust me to catch you." Cautiously, but obediently, Bryan jumped into his daddy's arms.

About four months later, Bryan was climbing a tree at a park. When it was time to go, Eddie reached out his arms to Bryan and quietly said, "Jump." To Eddie's astonishment, Bryan joyfully jumped into the arms of his loving father. Trust had been developed by choosing to trust. . . .

Most of the disappointment and pain we have suffered have come from misplaced trust. We have loved God and trusted people. Some of those people have violated our trust. Now we must learn to trust God and love people![1]

What is the central verse in the Bible? I'm talking about the verse that falls in the middle, with an equal number of verses before and after. My instinct says this verse should be especially significant, and here is what I found:

It is better to trust in the LORD than to put confidence in man (Ps. 118:8).

As if to underscore His point, God says in the next verse:

It is better to trust in the LORD than to put confidence in princes (Ps. 118:9).

Could it be that the people who have brought us the most disappointment weren't really our problem after all? Sure, they may have hurt us, but is it possible that the greater sin was our expectations of them? We weren't supposed to put our trust in them. We were to *love* them and to trust God.

What about your trust in God? Does your prayer life indicate your trust in Him, or are you praying anxiety-ridden, worry-filled prayers? God wants you to pray confident prayers based on who you know Him to be and what you know Him to have promised.

Trust is absolutely necessary for any deep and abiding relationship with God. In fact, it is the doorway to intimacy with Him. Has your trust been damaged because you misplaced it by trusting someone to do something or to be someone that he or she refused to do or be? I'm sure you found it hard to trust the next time around. If so, you must grab hold of your trust and place it squarely in your unfailing, unconditionally loving Father in heaven.

Pause here for a moment. Then take a deep breath and prepare yourself for a revelation: God Himself has allowed men to fail you in order to teach you to trust Him alone. He is jealous of your trust. He says, "For you shall worship no other god, for the LORD, whose name is Jealous, is a jealous God" (Exod. 34:14). Wow! Did you hear that? His name is Jealous! He is seriously committed to receiving our trust—so committed, in fact, that He guarantees our misplaced trust-based relationships will fail so that we will finally learn to place our trust in Him alone (see Ezek. 13:10-15).

Why do you think this is true? Because He is the only one who will *never* fail us. God is the only one who will *never* let us down. Even those who love us most will hurt us from time to time. Not the Father! He is completely trustworthy. Our failure to trust Him is a miserable sin. It is the sin of unbelief. You may say, *I'm just cautious; you can never be too careful, you know.* Perhaps. But many of us use those words to disguise our unbelief. The sad truth is that we have never learned to put our trust in God alone. Solomon's words give godly counsel:

> Trust in the LORD with all your heart, and lean not on your own understanding; in all your ways acknowledge Him, and He shall direct your paths (Prov. 3:5-6).

Will you trust the Lord to hold you, to love you, to heal you? Will you jump into His loving arms? Others will continue to disappoint you, but you can trust the Lord. He will not let you fall. Guaranteed!

Note
1. Alice Smith, *Beyond the Veil* (Ventura, CA: Regal Books, 1997), pp. 125-126.

Moorings of Our Journey

When He had stopped speaking, He said to Simon,
"Launch out into the deep and let down
your nets for a catch."

LUKE 5:4

Many of us prefer to keep our boats safely tied to the pier rather than launch out into the deep with Christ. To be sure, when a boat is tied to the pier, it is sheltered within the harbor; the wind is calm and the water is smooth. But boats are designed for sailing, not docking. The boating adventure begins out in the open sea with the wind and the salty ocean spray in your face.

The same is true of your spiritual journey with the Lord. If, like most people, you are content to stay in port, tied to the dock, then you will have limited opportunity to know Him. However, if you intend to discover who He truly is and your destiny in Him, then cast off your moorings in faith and launch out into the deep with Him. If you will forsake your fears and risk a deeper intimacy with Jesus, then you will learn more about Him; and in the vast ocean of His Spirit, you will find the very desire of your heart.

Simon Peter was so anxious to experience the supernatural power of Christ that when he and other disciples who were in a boat saw Jesus walking toward them on water tossed by waves from a contrary wind, he asked:

> "Lord, if it is You, command me to come to You on the water." So He said, "Come." And when Peter had come down out of the boat, he walked on the water to go to Jesus (Matt. 14:28-29).

But something happened to Peter in the process. The text tells us:

> But when [Peter] saw that the wind was boisterous, he was afraid; and beginning to sink he cried out, saying, "Lord, save me!" And immediately Jesus stretched out His hand and caught him, and said to him, "O you of little faith, why did you doubt?" (Matt 14:30-31).

Facing life's trials is a lot like launching out into the deep or stepping out of the boat. When we've finally risked enough to step out and then find ourselves confronted with overwhelming odds, we immediately cry out for Jesus to deliver us. The Lord is saying, "I want to do more than deliver you. I want to develop you."

Even in the test that Satan prepared for Peter we can see how Jesus was trying to develop Peter's character. "And the Lord said, 'Simon, Simon! Indeed, Satan has asked for you, that he may sift you as wheat. But I have prayed for you'" (Luke 22:31-32). Surely Peter must have been shocked to hear of Satan's plan to sift him, but I'm sure he was relieved that Jesus had prayed for him. By now Simon Peter knew that the Father always heard and answered Jesus' prayers. What could Peter have possibly thought when he discovered that Jesus had not prayed for the relief of sifting? Rather, Jesus said, "I have prayed for you, that your faith should not fail; and when you have returned to Me, strengthen your brethren" (Luke 22:32). Jesus prayed only that Simon

Peter's faith would stand the test and that the test would strengthen him.

You, too, will be tested. The wind and the waves of the open sea are designed to test your commitment to the Lord. He wants you to have more than a shallow experience with Him; He wants you to know His depths. A deep relationship with God requires deep testing, and deep testing requires deep faith. The Lord designs and tailors our testing so that we might earn the right of passage to walk with Him at deeper levels.

The psalmist said, "O God of my righteousness: thou hast enlarged me when I was in distress" (Ps. 4:1, *KJV*). If the Lord harbored you at the same, safe place all your life, you would never grow. He periodically calls you to launch out into the deep, to step out of the boat and face life's storms with Him. If you refuse to trust Jesus and risk the journey, then you will never know the joy of deep intimacy with Him. In this untested condition you may remain unfit for His service and possibly never reach your destiny.

Yet if you will step out of the boat and test the water, you will learn who God is and who you are, and your faith will grow under the pressure. These experiences will develop a Christlike sensitivity and sympathy for others who are facing life's hardships. You know what they are going through, for you have been there, too.

Intimate with the Father

*I love the LORD, because He has heard my
voice and my supplications.*

PSALM 116:1

*O*f all the things He [God] reveals to us, nothing is more precious, nothing is more relational than the revelation of Himself. He is under no obligation to share Himself with us, but He does. As our heavenly Lover reveals the hidden secrets of His heart, we are deeply affected. Having our senses deadened daily to the "self-life" (Rom. 6:11), our spirit is magnetically drawn into the vast ocean of His love. Amazingly, God invites us to Himself.[1]

I've often said that the Father has no favorites but He does have intimates. Jesus loved all of His disciples, including Judas. But John described himself as the "disciple whom Jesus loved" (John 21:7). It was Peter, James and John who accompanied Jesus to the mount of transfiguration. These were the men who longed to have a closer relationship with Him.

The Lord wants intimacy with us more than we want intimacy with Him. He is looking for people from all walks of life—homemakers, lawyers, dot-comers, plumbers, doctors, bankers, teachers—who will spend quality time with Him. He can only share His heart with those who delight to be in His presence in the place of prayer.

If you are an intercessor, you should know that the foundation of effective intercession is love, and the foundation of love is intimacy. Intercession is not *a work* to be done; it is a *relationship* to be developed. The more time we spend alone with the Father, the more intimately we will know Him. Moses knew the ways of God when others of his generation only knew God's deeds. They knew what God had done, but Moses knew why God did it (see Ps. 103:7)! David, God's worshiping warrior, was known as a man after God's own heart. Why? Because, like Moses, David prayed for God to show him His ways (see Exod. 33:13; Ps. 25:4).

The deeper the level of intimacy you enjoy with the Lord, the more confident in Christ you will become, until you are settled and secure in His love. And you will come to love Him more. After all, you can't love someone you hardly know.

Intimacy with Christ will transcend your intellect, which is part of your fallenness. Intimacy connects you spirit to Spirit and heart to heart. Many Christians mistake performance for God in public as a test of their effectiveness. However, our spiritual effectiveness will ultimately be determined by the measure of our private communion with the Lord.

There are many Christians who are content just to know that they will go to heaven when they die. They are content to have memorized a few Bible verses to lean on. They are content to tip God each week at offering time when they drop by church for their weekly obligatory visit. Heaven forbid! That's living life in a rut. And someone has said that a rut is a grave with both ends knocked out!

This intimacy I describe may sound intimidating if as a child you experienced traumatic incidents from a father figure. To develop an intimate relationship with Christ will require that you knock down the walls of protection you have built around your heart and become vulnerable all over again. The heavenly Father will never hurt or abuse you; you can depend on that. Guard your heart against the popular "victimization theology" that is sweeping through the Christian Church. As one who knows, I assure you that you can rise above the pain, draw intimately close to the Lord and live in victory. And know this: Although past hurts should not hinder you from enjoying closeness with Christ, intimacy with Christ will heal your past hurts!

Will you content yourself with only being acquainted with Christ? When next you find yourself in prayer, simply bask in His presence. Spend quality time bragging on Him. Tell Jesus what you appreciate about Him. As you approach Him with all of your defenses down, He will tenderly father you and fashion you into His likeness. Who better to transform you than the Lover of your soul?

Note

1. Alice Smith, *Beyond the Veil* (Ventura, CA: Regal Books, 1997), p. 155.

The Bride of Christ

For I am jealous for you with godly jealousy. For I have betrothed you to one husband, that I may present you as a chaste virgin to Christ.

2 CORINTHIANS 11:2

When God saw Adam alone in the garden, He said, "It is not good." Using a rib from Adam's side, God formed a bride and named her Eve—the mother of all humankind. Have you ever thought of the fact that at the very moment the Father prepared a bride for Adam, He was also preparing a Bride for His Son, Jesus? For every nation, tribe and tongue has its origin in Eve; and from every nation, tribe and tongue, the heavenly Father has formed Jesus' Bride, the Church. The Church encompasses the beauty of every race and culture.

During Old Testament times, a common place to seek a bride was at the local well. Women gathered every day at this source of physical sustenance to draw water for their families (see Gen. 24 for the story of Rebekah at the well). Spiritually speaking, for our spiritual sustenance, we must continually go to Jesus, who is the pure source of living water that sustains our souls. All too often, however, instead of finding sustenance directly from the source, Jesus' Bride drinks from tainted streams to fill her spiritual thirst with religious activity. Going to church or even joining a church, however, is not the well of refreshment. Jesus Himself is the well of living water that will refresh the Bride. Jesus wants to fill the thirst of His Bride with pure and clean water. He said, "Whoever believes in me, as the Scripture has said, streams of living water will flow from within him" (John 7:38, *NIV*).

What does it mean to be Jesus' Bride—to be one with Him? Because we were chosen to be in Christ from the foundation of the world, when Jesus died, we died. And when Jesus was in the grave, so were we. When Jesus was resurrected from the dead, so were we! That's why Paul could write to the Romans, "Knowing this, that our old man was crucified with Him. Likewise you also, reckon yourselves to be dead indeed to sin, but alive to God in Christ Jesus our Lord" (Rom. 6:6,11). Think of it! God's plan for a Bride—the Father's desire for an intimate relationship with us in a divinely designed marriage—was dependent upon Christ's resurrection from the dead! That thought alone should stoke the fire of our love for our Bridegroom. But why should we need to stoke the fire?

Just as we are enamored with our lover and life partner in the days of courtship and early in marriage, after the days turn to months and the months to years, the flames of passion can die down to smoldering embers. One day the two lovers are shocked to realize how much they have filled their days with activities that have caused them to drift apart. They have forgotten the most important fact of their relationship—their love for each other.

So it is with our relationship with Christ. We are prone to forget our love for our Bridegroom. We become careless; we get busy and distracted and make our heavenly Lover wait for us to return to Him. As the Bride of Christ, we are going to be judged not for what we have done but for why we have done it, not for what we failed to do but for why we didn't do it. How, then, can we stay close to the Lord?

One thing we can do is to trust Him fully. In my anxious

moments, I find myself wanting to know what the Lord is doing and why He is doing it. But He invites me to learn only about who He is. The Lord refuses to tell me the specifics about what He is doing. By getting to know Him, I learn His character and then I am able to discern His ways. I have found that those who know God's ways know His heart; those who know His acts know only His hand. I want to know His ways, don't you?

> When the inner spirit plunges into the fathomless ocean of God's love, consummation of a divine union has occurred. Male or female, all are one in Christ. The Bride and her heavenly Groom are one. This relationship is like a sweet perfume that fills the air. In the life of this new partnership, the human spirit experiences the joy of forgiveness, and the assurance of life eternal. An awakening of the inner life has occurred.
>
> During the honeymoon phase of any new marriage, love is immature. . . . The same is true when we begin our relationship with Jesus. We depend heavily on His reinforcing love. As the relationship deepens, however, we learn to give our love to Him more freely.[1]

It is in falling in love with Jesus, the Son of God, again and again, that we learn of Him and become a fit helpmeet for our Bridegroom. Will you renew your love for Him today?

Note

1. Alice Smith, *Beyond the Veil* (Ventura, CA: Regal Books, 1997), p. 150.

Time to Burn the Incense

*So it was, that while he was serving as priest before God
in the order of his division, according to the custom
of the priesthood, his lot fell to burn incense
when he went into the temple of the Lord.*

LUKE 1:8-9

You might remember from Luke 1 that Zechariah and Elizabeth, John the Baptist's parents, were "righteous before God" (v. 6). Both were descended from the priestly tribe of Aaron, advanced in years, yet barren. In the same way, the Church today is a kingdom of priests (see Rev. 1:5-6), advanced in years—having had 2,000 years to learn the priestly skills—and yet essentially barren—powerless and fruitless.[1]

Luke records that Zechariah's priestly division was assigned to temple duty when they drew the lot to burn the incense (see Luke 1:8-9). Imagine being chosen from a pool of approximately 22,000 active priests. This was a once-in-a-lifetime opportunity! Verse 10 tells us that as the priest burned the incense, multitudes of people were praying outside the Temple, for it was "the time of incense" (*KJV*).[2]

Just as Zechariah burned the incense before the first coming of Jesus, I believe our generation has drawn the lot to burn the incense before Christ's second coming! Around the world, multitudes are praying! Those who burn the incense will become saturated with the fragrance of intercession that ascends pleasantly before Him. And as they do, they will experience life the way God intended it: connected and satisfied by Him inside the Holy of Holies. Then when people who are living in the outer court and the world experience the fragrance of His lingering presence, they will be aroused and unsatisfied with strange fire and counterfeit incense. They will long for that place known as the Holy of Holies.[3]

My husband, Eddie, has an anointing to lead people into the presence of God through worship like no other person I know. It is not unusual when we teach and Eddie is asked to sing a solo or lead congregational worship that the audience is crying by the end of the worship time.

When Eddie was the worship leader of our church in the 1980s, our praise and worship were so glorious that at times the congregation couldn't even stand on their feet. One particular night we had worshiped for 45 minutes in what seemed like the timeless presence of the Lord. When I opened my eyes, I could actually see a cloud hovering over the congregation. I could see in the midst of the thin white cloud a few hands that were uplifted, and the legs of some people, but the glory cloud was over us. I don't know if anyone else experienced this amazing phenomenon, but that night there wasn't a dry eye in the building. No sermon could be preached. Our awareness of God's glory was so present that somehow we all knew that the worst thing we could do would be to speak. Some people sat in their chairs while others lay on the floor. Many people remained standing. We all sensed His divine visitation that evening.

There is a reason for this kind of visitation: The Father is drawing us into the Holy of Holies to restore the ministry of intercession today. Because of His prophetic end-time purposes—as well as for the desperate need of our generation—He is calling us into our prayer closets. No other generation has lived so close to the brink of annihilation as ours.

God is looking for two kinds of people. He is looking for those who will worship Him in spirit and in truth (see John 4:23), and He is looking for those who will stand in the gap to intercede for the land (see Ezek. 22:30). He longs for worshipers and intercessors who will give themselves away in intercessory prayer.

In heaven, there are 24 elders surrounding God's throne. Of them Scripture records: "Each one had a harp and they were holding golden bowls full of incense, which are the prayers of the saints" (Rev. 5:8, *NIV*). When we get serious about prayer, then the tears, fasting and travail of our intercession will cause the golden bowls full of incense in heaven to overflow:

> Another angel, who had a golden censer, came and stood at the altar. He was given much incense to offer, with the prayers of all the saints, on the golden altar before the throne. The smoke of the incense, together with the prayers of the saints, went up before God from the angel's hand (Rev. 8:3-4, *NIV*).

No doubt the cup of man's sin is full and the judgment of God is approaching. I encourage you to answer God's call to intercede—to step boldly into the Holy of Holies where His presence engulfs you. As you do this, the burden on the Father's heart will become the focus of your prayers. Open your heart to receive a God-sized view of our world, and unite your heart with others to make a difference in prayer. Only then will you taste the joys of heaven and see millions of people prayed into the kingdom of God. Can you sense the urgency of the hour? Your prayers count! The golden bowls at heaven's altar—collecting the prayers of God's people—are almost full.

Pray right now:

Father, I am your priest chosen to intercede for my generation.
I am asking, Lord, that my prayers and my life will be
as a sweet incense before your throne. I rededicate my life to
you today. In Jesus' name, amen.

Notes
1. Alice Smith, *Beyond the Veil* (Ventura, CA: Regal Books, 1997), p. 99.
2. Ibid.
3. Ibid.

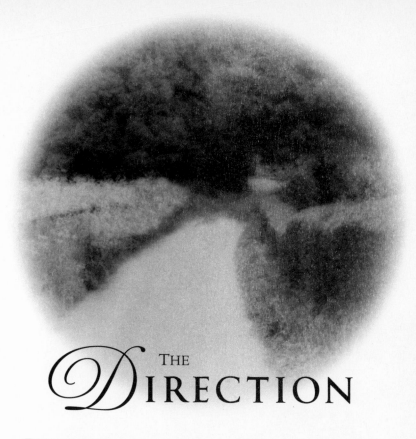

The DIRECTION

DIRECTION: THE COURSE ALONG WHICH A PERSON
MOVES TOWARD A PARTICULAR GOAL.

*Every journey needs a map. Our journey into intimacy
with God is no exception. Now that we know our
intended destination, let me show you the various routes
into God's presence. Not long from now you will
become familiar with the journey and move along well-
traveled routes beyond the veil.*

Can You Pass the Test?

Beloved, do not think it strange concerning the fiery trial which is to try you, as though some strange thing happened to you.

1 PETER 4:12

At the beginning of a college course, one professor gave his students the 100 answers to his final exam and told them they would be required to know the answers by the end of the semester. His fellow professors were angry and accused him of cheating his students by providing them with the answers before the test was given. His reply: "My goal is to teach them this subject. These 100 questions contain the essence of the subject. If at the end of the course they can recall these answers, then they have learned what I am paid to teach them."

The students of the other professors had no idea what their teachers' goals were or what would constitute mastery of the material. They didn't have a clue what was going to be asked on the final exam in their classes. They didn't know what to take note of, what to remember or what to be prepared to answer until the last few days (if then) before the exam.

Aren't we glad that God gives us the answers *before* the test? His Word, His Spirit and the life experiences of others tutor us so that we can pass our tests. In one sense, although we may not know the route the Lord will use to get us where He is taking us, we can know the destination. In that sense, we are able to know the end at the beginning.

When I was in college, many of us would stay up all night to read our textbooks, look over our notes and cram for our exams. We could only guess what questions the teacher might ask on the test. Some of the girls would actually go to bed early. What was wrong with them? Didn't they care about their grades? The final result, however, was that some of them scored better than those of us who had crammed all night. Why? Because their minds were rested and clear enough to recall the right answers!

As Christians we need to release all anxiety. Anyone can imagine the negative "what if's" of life, but anxiety will blind us to what is right in front of us. Things may seem clear enough, but then the test results are posted. We knew the answer, but our anxiety caused us to miss it.

Never make important decisions when you are distressed and unable to see clearly. When you are calm and collected, however, you will find the will of God more clearly revealed. If you are feeling anxious, turn from your problem and focus your thoughts on praise and devotion. Listen to the Lord and forget self-condemnation. In that place of inner quietness, your mind relaxes and your spirit is freed to commune with the Holy Spirit. It is here that He reveals the truth and gives you wisdom to make good decisions.

Let's face it, life is complicated! It's easy to get worked up into a frenzy when your baby is sick, you've lost your job, the money is tight and your marriage is stressed. Pressure hinders your ability to think, much less pray effectively. As the pressure builds, you may find yourself speaking hurtful words that only exacerbate the situation. Never trust your immediate impulses during these pressured times.

An experienced spiritual counselor will warn you to hold off making important decisions until you regain your inner calm.

Slow down. Turn inward to your heart. Hear yourself praising the Lord. Remind Him of His goodness and the good things He has done and will do. "Give yourself to the LORD; trust in him, and he will help you" (Ps. 37:5, *TEV*). As you give yourself completely to praise, your anxiety will dissipate.

God allows tests to come into our lives. Testing is not the time to forsake the journey of knowing Him more! The point of testing is to please the Lord in every decision you make. If you persist in pushing through with your own decisions when it is time to reflect and wait for His voice, then failure is certain.

James 1:2 says, "My brethren, count it all joy when you fall into various trials." This verse is so interesting to me. The word "count" means to line up in a column or in a row. A paraphrase would be: Line up in the column of joy when various kinds of trials come your way. Imagine yourself jumping up and down with your hands in the air, shouting, "Lord, let me be the one to go through the test!"

Tests come to us not to inform God about our situation but to help us know Him and ourselves better. God has already given us the answers to our test; now He wants us to take the test so that we can prove to ourselves and to others that we know the answers. Are you ready?

A Lifestyle of Commitment

His lord said to him, "Well done, good and faithful servant;
you have been faithful over a few things, I will make you
ruler over many things. Enter into the joy of your lord."

MATTHEW 25:23

Robert, our oldest son, is an anointed worship leader and is developing a recording studio. I couldn't be more proud of all that God has done in his life. Not only is Robert a skillful guitarist, but he also writes, records and leads congregational worship.

It wasn't always this way. As all children must do, Robert had to make the choice whether or not he would serve the Lord. We can teach our children right from wrong and how to honor and love God; but as they grow toward maturity, the choice becomes theirs to apply what they have been taught. One of the most difficult challenges for a parent is to watch a child make wrong choices. Eddie and I have certainly faced this challenge with our own children. The pain can go deeper than one can describe; and unless you have experienced a child's rebellion, it is sometimes easier to judge than to understand.

Like his dad, Robert has always been very musical; it seemed to be a given that he would use that gifting in some way. When the time was right, Robert decided to do his own thing and start a rock band. He struggled financially to make ends meet and made many wrong choices. But nothing calmed his restlessness, and nothing ever would. He tried to run from God's calling on his life, but everywhere he turned the heavenly Father was there with open arms to receive him back. Aren't you glad we serve a merciful and loving God? He is always ready and willing to help us in our time of trouble.

After several years, Eddie decided to write a letter to Robert, inviting him to come back home. The conditions were that Robert would work full-time, get out of debt and let us teach him how to live for the Lord. We were so excited when Robert called and said yes. When our son drove into our driveway, it was clear that the devil hadn't paid very well. All of Robert's earthly possessions were on the backseat! The car was old and almost ready for the junk pile. But our precious son was now a broken man, ready for God's intervention.

The day Robert came home, Eddie was leaving to attend a worship conference in Dallas, Texas, and he invited Robert to go with him. One night at the hotel during the conference, Eddie went to the room while Robert stayed in the lobby to talk on the phone. As Eddie walked into the room, he began to hear a new song in his heart and quickly pulled out a piece of music manuscript paper to notate a 16-measure worship song. He folded the paper, placed it in his Bible and turned on the television to watch the 10 o'clock news.

About 20 minutes later, Robert arrived and said, "Dad, do you have any music paper? I have an idea for a song." Eddie said, "Sure. Look in the top drawer." When Robert finished writing, he said, "Well, I have it written, but I don't have any words for it yet." Eddie said, "Son, let me see what you've written." When he looked at the paper, he could hardly believe his eyes: Robert's song was exactly the same 16-measure melody as Eddie's and was even written in the same key!

Eddie said, "Son, I think you'll find the words in my Bible." When Robert pulled out his dad's song, his eyes got big. "Dad, how did we both write the same song?!" he exclaimed. Eddie dryly answered, "The Lord did it." "Yeah, but how did it happen?" Robert insisted. Eddie again said, "Son, the Lord did it."

Not to be stopped, Robert said, "Dad, if you put a thousand songwriters in a room and asked them to write a 16-measure song, no two of them would be alike."

"Unless . . . " Eddie began.

"Unless what?" Robert said.

"Unless God did it."

"Okay, if God did it, then why did He do it?" Robert asked.

"Son, God allowed this miracle to happen to show both of us how He is going to use you. It is heaven's confirmation of who you are and what you've been called to do."

The Lord has done great things in Robert. But one of the noticeable things I can see in him every day is his gratitude to God for bringing him out of the world. Robert learned how to defeat the devil at his own game, and he became a man of integrity.

Even with a decision to surrender to God, more is needed. King Saul had great abilities and a genuine calling, but he lacked integrity. As a result, his leadership failed in the end. Ultimately, God is more interested in *who we are* than in *what we do*. Only a person with integrity will be able to withstand the plans of the enemy in these last days. That's loyalty!

Are you so thankful for the work God has done in your life that you are committed to a lifestyle of integrity and loyalty to Jesus?

Power Encounter

And He said to me, "My grace is sufficient for you, for My strength is made perfect in weakness." Therefore most gladly I will rather boast in my infirmities, that the power of Christ may rest upon me. Therefore I take pleasure in infirmities, in reproaches, in needs, in persecutions, in distresses, for Christ's sake. For when I am weak, then I am strong.

2 CORINTHIANS 12:9-10

I was in my early twenties when Eddie and I went to a denominational convention in Dallas, Texas, and had the opportunity to meet two giants in the faith: Dr. Leonard Ravenhill, the revivalist who wrote *Why Revival Tarries,* and Miss Bertha Smith, a straight-shooting Southern Baptist missionary who served alongside Rev. Hudson Taylor during China's Shantung Revival. They were both keynote speakers. Miss Bertha retired in 1958 and died at the age of 100.

One night during the conference, the late Reverend Manley Beasley, our spiritual father, invited us to a prayer meeting held in a hotel room near the convention center. Eddie and I were pleased to accept his invitation. I thought to myself, *This will be fun,* since I knew some things about prayer and felt qualified to be a part of the group. However, my zeal for God outweighed my knowledge of His ways. Unfortunately, I was about to see the truth concerning my spiritual condition.

The experience is almost as real to me today as it was that warm night in 1973. As Manley, Eddie and I approached the hotel room, I felt what I can only describe as waves of God's anointing in the hallway. From the room we could hear moans and groans and loud crying from those already gathered in the hotel room. Their wailing was so intense that you would have thought someone was torturing them. My earlier confidence started to change into uneasiness. I was young in the things of God, even though I was hungry for more of Him.

When we opened the door, words cannot fully describe what I saw. The room was stiflingly hot. In the soft glow of two or three table lamps, I saw men and women laid out on the floor, sprawled across the bed, leaning up against the windows and walls, all in agony of soul. Dr. Ravenhill passionately prayed for each of us to surrender our lives to God. He fervently prayed for the Lord to rend the heavens and bring a great awakening to America. His voice thundered with power and conviction. I dropped quickly to my knees, for I didn't have enough strength to walk any further into the room. The anointing of God was so powerful that my heart raced and I found it hard to breathe.

Every prayer of Leonard Ravenhill and Miss Bertha cut like a knife into our hearts. I remember that as one pastor began to pray the words, "Lord, if I have sinned, would you—" Miss Bertha abruptly interrupted him midsentence and said, "Son, what do you mean, 'if I have sinned?' You know you're a sinner—now you get honest with God!" The poor pastor broke into tears, repenting of all kinds of things that I don't remember now. I was stunned. The power of God in that prayer meeting was unlike anything I had ever experienced before! Revival broke out in that room that night. I, too, began to weep over my sin. Heaven was touching Earth!

What does my recollection of an awesome prayer time over 30 years ago mean for you? Simply this: Our God is a trigenerational God—the God of Abraham, Isaac and Jacob. Your anointing will be equal to or even greater than the anointing of those who have gone before you. In fact, you *should* experience a greater anointing since you are able to stand on the spiritual foundation those who have gone before you have laid. I am a better Christian because of the experiences I learned from my spiritual elders. Each succeeding generation should stand on the spiritual strengths of the one that came before. Resist the urge to compare yourself with others, just as Paul warned: "For we dare not class ourselves or compare ourselves with those who commend themselves. But they, measuring themselves by themselves, and comparing themselves among themselves, are not wise" (2 Cor. 10:12).

Someone once asked Hudson Taylor, "Why do you suppose God chose you to help lead the Shantung revival?" Reverend Taylor thought for a moment and then answered wisely, "I suppose He just looked around until he found someone weak enough."

You are here for one purpose only: to glorify God. Christ in you is your only hope of glory (see Col. 1:27). Keep reading, because the Word delivers great news: You are complete in Christ (see Col. 2:10) and He has given you everything you need for godly living (see 2 Pet. 1:3). God never calls the equipped; He always equips the called. And now it is your turn to touch the younger generation with your passion and your prayers.

Receiving Correction

For exaltation comes neither from the east nor from the west nor from the south. But God is the Judge: He puts down one, and exalts another.

PSALM 75:6-7

Can you give away something that you don't have? Of course you can't! Yet we somehow have the idea that we can consecrate our unsurrendered lives to the Lord. There is only one thing we can wholly give to the Lord: the right to ourselves (see Rom. 12)!

In God's character-building school, there is a basic operational principle: If when we are tested, challenged, corrected or rebuked, we choose to receive the correction with grace and humility, then the Lord will continue to promote us. But once we get bitter, take offense or try to defend our rights, then the Lord registers our reaction and sees that we are not ready for any higher position of authority. Why? Because surely we couldn't handle the criticism and pressure that comes with more responsibility.

God tested King David's reaction to correction through the words of the prophet Nathan. When David and the beautiful Bathsheba had hardly risen from their bed of adultery, David made arrangements for her husband, his faithful military officer Uriah, to be killed on the front line of battle (see 2 Sam. 11:14-27). It seemed that David had now cunningly arranged his world to make allowances for his sin. But God says, "Be sure your sin will find you out" (Num. 32:23).

Following the time of mourning Uriah's death, God sent His prophet Nathan to confront King David with his sin (see 2 Sam. 12). Nathan told David a story about a poor man with one sheep—a family pet. He explained how a rich man stole and ate the poor man's only sheep. Thinking that the story was true, King David grew incensed and demanded that the rich man be arrested and immediately executed for such a thoughtless and selfish act. Calmly, Nathan told David that the story was a parable about David's own life. The prophet turned to David and said: "You are the man!" (v. 7).

How would David, who had unlimited power in his kingdom, respond to Nathan's accusation? Would he turn his anger toward Nathan and have him executed instead? Would he deny his sin with Bathsheba? Would he ignore his sin and continue living his life of royalty?

Amazingly, David immediately repented and openly confessed his sin. His words still echo through the halls of history: "I have sinned against the LORD" (v. 13). David obviously was a man of integrity. He accepted with grace the correction due him. He didn't want to compound his sin of backsliding by adding to it the sin of hypocrisy.

No one enjoys correction. Facing discipline is never fun. In fact, it can be quite painful. Sometimes the criticism is justified, but other times it isn't. But correction is sometimes necessary if we are to remain spiritually healthy. To listen and heed correction builds our character and often opens the door to future opportunities. The person who is spiritually unteachable will go back to address the same issues over and over again until he or she learns to receive correction with grace and humility.

The discipline may come in an incorrect manner, but that is not the issue at hand. The question is, When you are challenged, corrected, rebuked or even misunderstood, what do you do? How do you respond? Do you snap back a retort and defend yourself? Do you lash out and point the finger at another? Do you sulk, run away or make excuses for your behavior? These are common responses, to be sure. However, in every correction there is a kernel of truth. Find that truth, permit the Lord to change your character, and see how the devil will be unable to find a way to accuse you. God wants to see you react supernaturally to these provocations. If you learn to receive correction with grace and humility, then promotion may be the next step in your future.

I was a church leader, Sunday School teacher and pastor's wife in the 1980s. I received an interesting challenge one day. I really didn't know Suzy very well when she walked up to me and said, "Alice, you have the anointing of Moses, but you lack the gentleness of Jesus." Suzy then spun around and walked away! *What?* I thought to myself, *Just who does she think she is?*

I have always submitted to prayer every criticism that comes my way. I did the same with this criticism. When I went to prayer, I began to argue with the Lord about what Suzy had said. I was shocked when I heard the Father speak to my heart, "Alice, Suzy is right." Immediately, I confessed this to the Lord and asked Him to change my character. Within a week, I went back to Suzy and told her the story. I hugged her and thanked her for the opportunity to be changed. To this day when I see her, I remind her of how the Father used that timely correction to build my character. Since then I have allowed the sometimes painful correction of others to help purify my life. How about you? Will you receive correction and be changed today?

Seasons of Life

You will show me the path of life; in Your presence is fullness of joy; at Your right hand are pleasures forevermore.

PSALM 16:11

Have you ever experienced such deep hurt that you were almost paralyzed with pain? The great Charles H. Spurgeon, in his devotional masterpiece *Days of Darkness*, wrote, "The dearest of his children must bear the cross. No Christian has enjoyed perpetual prosperity. . . . We need winds and tempests to exercise our faith, to tear off the rotten bough of self-dependence, and to root us more firmly in Christ."[1]

Conflict brings to the surface what is not of God. Our flesh nature is usually the first to respond to hurt and reveals our self-love. Once we recognize the difference between the flesh and the spirit, we are able to recognize the signs of death operating in us. We can fully recognize death in our flesh by the "stink," because nothing fresh is coming from us.

God promises us that His mercies are new every morning (see Lam. 3:23). When God produced manna to feed the children of Israel during their desert wandering, the manna appeared fresh every morning. It had an extremely short shelf life; it became stale in only one day. In the same way, our faith requires a resurrection every morning; yesterday's victories will not sustain us for today's challenges. We need new revelation each day.

Life's difficulties should remind us that death to self is necessary for our sanctification. Our separation from soulishness is like a snake shedding its skin—uncomfortable but necessary.

When the old skin drops off, there is new soft skin in its place. Our soul has to experience a similar sloughing off so that it won't hinder our spiritual development.

Thankfully, there are stages in our spiritual life when we won't experience any storms. Yet when a crisis does arise, our response will instantly reveal upon whom we are relying. If we have been learning to worship and trust the Lord, even though the crisis takes us to the breaking point, we will not break. Our confidence in the Father will not fail. Sanctification will have its way in us. Our oneness with the Lord will allow us to rest in Him, and our ability to rest in the Lord will bring joy to His heart and healing to our own.

Did you know that the Christian life is seasonal? That's right. Just as the earth experiences winter, spring, summer and fall, you, too, will have seasons in your spiritual life. In the autumn season the days grow shorter and cooler; the leaves begin to change color and fall as the ground becomes dormant. You, too, will experience a fall season when the motions of your relationship with Christ begin to cool. That's when the Father will begin to purge your soul and the dead things in your life will fall away. Your prayer time will focus on personal sin and the acknowledgment of character flaws that need to change.

Then there is the winter of your Christian walk when everything around you feels dead. The spiritual ground is frozen hard. Meaningful prayer seems almost impossible. You struggle to hear the Lord speak. Dormancy comes. Don't despair; this is normal. Although your mind isn't able to conjure up prayer activity, your heart is eager to tune in to hear His voice. The important thing to do is remain faithful in the winter of your life.

During springtime the flowers begin to bloom, grass grows, the air is fresh, and birds sing. There is new life everywhere. In your spiritual springtime, the Word of God comes alive to you and revelation is fresh once more. Joy floods your heart.

And then you experience the summer. Prophecy comes alive as the brightness of God's glory surrounds you. Worship is powerful and His voice is strong and clear.

Are you in a time of trouble today? Have hurts invaded your life? Do you feel numb, almost dead in your heart? Are you asking, Where is the Lord? If He doesn't seem to be speaking, don't be discouraged. "If you faint in the day of adversity, your strength is small" (Prov. 24:10). Your natural inclination is to struggle, strain and strive. My friend, this is the test of your faith. This is your exam. The teacher never talked when proctoring an exam, and so it is with the Lord. God never talks during the test. But once the test is over, He will comfort your troubled soul. There is no need to be anxious. It is a win-win situation. Sometimes the Lord calms the storm, and sometimes He calms His child in the midst of the storm.

When you process the seasons of life properly by focusing on Christ and His glory, you will past the test—with integrity as the result. Without tests, you will never see the Lord. If you never see the Lord, you will never reach your destiny in Him.

Rather than defend yourself today, embrace humility. Then you will grow in the grace of God and He will fight for you!

Note

1. Charles H. Spurgeon, "Daily Devotionals," *Days of Darkness*. http://www. heartlight.org/spurgeon/0429-am.html (accessed May 21, 2003).

Wilderness

He who has begun a good work in you will complete it until the day of Jesus Christ.

PHILIPPIANS 1:6

When we're trekking through the wilderness, we are tempted to think, *The devil led me here.* However, it is the pathway through the wilderness that leads to intimacy with Jesus. God told Hosea, concerning Israel: "'Therefore, behold, I will allure her [Hosea's prostitute wife], will bring her into the wilderness, and speak comfort to her. I will give her her vineyards from there, and the Valley of Achor [trouble] as a door of hope; she shall sing there, as in the days of her youth, as in the day when she came up from the land of Egypt. And it shall be, in that day,' says the LORD, 'that you will call Me "My Husband," and no longer call Me "My Master"'" (Hos. 2:14-16).

The wilderness experience moves us from a master-servant relationship to a bride-and-groom relationship. The identifying marks of the wilderness are personal trials, the silence of God and the absence of His felt presence. This journey can also be a place of loneliness, darkness and, yes, even desperation. But if you remember that our journey in God is cyclical, then you can take courage from the fact that a wilderness experience always precedes divine revelation, and divine revelation always precedes breakthrough! And so the cycle goes: wilderness, then revelation, then breakthrough; wilderness . . . revelation . . . breakthrough.

We see this pattern repeatedly in Scripture. Consider Elijah, who instructed the false prophets to build an altar, stack firewood on it and offer an animal sacrifice, and then challenge Baal, their god, to consume it with fire. Nothing happened (see

1 Kings 18:26). Then Elijah teased them, saying, "Maybe your god has gone out of the country, or perhaps he is asleep" (see v. 27).

Then it was Elijah's turn. Three times he drenched the firewood and filled the trenches with water. "Then the fire of the LORD fell and consumed the burnt sacrifice, and the wood and the stones and the dust, and it licked up the water that was in the trench. Now when all the people saw it, they fell on their faces; and they said, 'The LORD, He is God! The LORD, He is God!'" (1 Kings 18:38-39).

Wow! That would have been something to see! A moment later Elijah single-handedly killed the 400 prophets of Baal and ascended victoriously to the top of the mountain to pray. The result? Rain began to fall, ending a three-year drought! Yet one chapter later we find this same powerful prophet running from Queen Jezebel. Scripture says that Elijah was afraid and ran for his life—into the desert (see 1 Kings 19:3-4). Elijah went from breakthrough to wilderness.

Jesus experienced the same kind of challenge. As John baptized Jesus, the Holy Spirit descended from heaven in the form of a dove, and God said, "You are My beloved Son; in You I am well pleased" (Luke 3:22). Then one chapter later, Jesus was led by the Holy Spirit into the wilderness to be tested (see Luke 4:1-2)!

Journeys through the wilderness precede breakthrough. We will all make the journey. So how can you prepare for your next wilderness experience? The prime prerequisite is to be filled with the Holy Spirit. Only Spirit-filled believers can be Spirit led. Only Spirit-led believers can live in the power of the Holy Spirit! Jesus was *led* into the wilderness *full* of the Holy Spirit (see Luke 4:1). Forty days later, Jesus emerged from the wilderness *in the power of* the Holy Spirit after He passed the wilderness test (see Luke 4:14).

The wilderness may present you with any number of tests, including financial problems, loss of a job, relational difficulties or even health problems. As Job learned, some of God's ways are more difficult to understand than others. They can include the death of a friend or family member or even the end of a marriage through divorce or death. Your wilderness journey may include the death of your life vision or ministry dream. No matter the circumstance, don't be defeated, for God is able to redeem every occurrence in your life.

What can you expect during a wilderness time? You will start with self-preservation and actually fight with the Lord on both the natural and the spiritual level. This is your attempt to pre-serve self-esteem. Your craving for legitimacy drives you to prove yourself to God, to others and to yourself. After all, American success is measured in terms of health and wealth. Aren't these visual proofs of God's approval? No! Health and wealth are man-made standards, not biblical ones. By these standards, the apostle Paul and Stephen would have been certifiable failures! One was sickly and in prison, without even a coat to wear. The other had his life cut short in his youth in a death by stoning.

Next you can expect that your mind will search for ways to correct the appearance that you are struggling. You will push to make things happen, but this only prolongs the fight. When you finally stop struggling, the result will be the defeat of your flesh and victory for your spirit. Your loss of self-confidence and your acquisition of God-dependence are evidence of the work of the wilderness in you. You now have a more honest evaluation of who you are to God and who He is to you. Praise the Lord, for revelation has produced breakthrough!

When the heavenly Father draws you into the wilderness and your circumstances become a wasteland and when everything appears to be turned upside down and you experience chaos to the very core of your being, get ready! It is here that your soul awakens to new revelation about yourself and your God. As you passionately pursue the Lord and His purposes and stand in faith on His promises, you will experience the depths of His mysterious love. After all, the river of God's love runs deepest in the valleys.

Necessity of Brokenness

*For I know the thoughts that I think toward you, says the
LORD, thoughts of peace, and not of evil, to give
you a future and a hope.*

JEREMIAH 29:11

Mr. and Mrs. Smith, your baby boy is dead. You see, the
child was growing deformed in your womb, and this is nature's
way of protecting you from the birth of a child that can't live in
this world. I am truly sorry. You are miscarrying the baby now."

When the doctor finished speaking, I looked at Eddie in disbelief. All the plans we had made for this child—gone! I wrestled
in prayer week after week about why the Father had allowed this
to happen. After many years I believe I have a small but important revelation about the pain we face in our walk with God.

It is like the story of Hansel and Gretel. The mean and cruel
stepfather leads them out to the wilderness to abandon them.
The children, fearful of losing their way, drop bread crumbs
along the path. When Hansel and Gretel run through the forest
looking for the crumbs they had strewn along the pathway, they
cannot find a single one. To their dismay, the birds had eaten the
bread. Now they were hopelessly lost—they couldn't find their
way home.

Does this sound familiar? We sometimes think the devil has
us on the path to destruction and God can't do anything about
it. We have dropped some bread crumbs along the way in our

Christian life, hoping that they will be the security we need to stay on track or keep a predictable path in life. Instead, we find that the birds have eaten our blessings. Because we are confused and unfamiliar with the ways of our heavenly Father, we actually fear a more intimate relationship with Him. The barriers spring up; we build walls and defenses. We have God in a box, or so we think. We begin to feel safe and in control. Our defenses relax and we assume that our world can go on as we have planned. But we soon become spiritually stagnant. We admit this is not what we want in our Christian lives. But what is the answer? How do we understand the ways of God and still fearlessly pursue Him? The answer is found in the mystery of brokenness.

Why does the Lord allow us to experience brokenness? All life is the result of some form of brokenness. The earth must be broken before the seed can be planted. The seed must be broken before the plant can grow. And the earth must once again be broken before new plant life can emerge from it. Brokenness then is a life-birthing process that must precede every area of growth in our lives. This is especially true as God develops our spiritual lives. Any spiritual fruitfulness will require the breaking from the outer person so that the spirit can commune with the Spirit of God in us.[1]

God uses broken things. Broken soil produces the crop, broken clouds produce the rain, broken grain makes the bread, and broken bread feeds the hungry. The decorative alabaster box is beautiful in its intricate design. Yet it is the broken alabaster box that releases its perfume for all to enjoy. It is a broken Simon Peter, weeping bitterly, who returns in apostolic power.

A God-designed path through brokenness brings each of us to death to self, which perfects our humility and releases our spirit-man (see Gal. 2:20). Jesus, our example, humbled Himself unto death. Paul, the apostle, said that he died daily (see 1 Cor.

15:31). Through brokenness the Holy Spirit empowers us to live the resurrected life. The fruit of brokenness that the Holy Spirit desires to produce in our lives is stronger godly character and personal integrity.

I am grateful for the ongoing breaking process in my own life. I have come to realize that brokenness is not my enemy; it is my friend. Scripture tells us that "a broken spirit, a broken and a contrite heart—these, O God, You will not despise" (Ps. 51:17). The brokenness the Lord is working in you isn't to break your spirit but to break the carnal nature of selfishness. When we are quick to humble ourselves and repent, then brokenness occurs and all resistance, independence and pride are replaced with submission, tenderness, obedience and love.

Is this your prayer today? The heavenly Father has a good plan for you. Part of that good plan is that the brokenness of your life will result in the sweet fragrance of His presence. You can trust Him in this process.

Note

1. Alice Smith, *Beyond the Veil* (Ventura, CA: Regal Books, 1997), pp. 129-130.

Building an Altar

Now I know that you fear God, since you have not withheld your son, your only son, from Me.

GENESIS 22:12

It happened one morning in 1970, around 2:30 A.M. In this prayer time, I began by reading a page from my favorite devotional book, and then I read a passage from the Bible. Next I lay on the floor to pray, where for the first 20 to 30 minutes I praised God for every detail of my life.

Suddenly this memorable prayer time in the wee hours of the morning was interrupted with a heavenly urge to let go—to let go of what, I wasn't sure. But the Spirit of the Lord was so strong in the room that I couldn't move from the floor. As I wept before Him, the Lord asked me, "Alice, where is the altar you have built for me?" I was confused until the Father reminded me of the life-changing altars that men in the Bible had built.

The Israelites feared the Baal-worshiping, mean-spirited Midianites who camped on their land and ruined their crops. So they cried out to God for help. One day, as Gideon threshed wheat in a winepress, an angel of the Lord spoke to him, saying, "The LORD is with you, mighty warrior" (Judg. 6:12, *NIV*). Gideon was confused. He reminded the angel that he was a small man and was considered the least in his clan. However, with a spark of unusual boldness, Gideon replied, "If now I have found favor in your eyes, give me a sign that it is really you talking to me. Please do not go away until I come back and bring my offering and set it before you" (vv. 17-18, *NIV*). And the Lord said, "I will wait until you return" (v. 18, *NIV*). Gideon prepared the meat and bread as the angel instructed and placed them on a rock. The angel then touched Gideon's offering with the tip of his staff and a flame from the rock consumed it. As the angel disappeared, Gideon was left with an overwhelming sense that he had just seen God face-to-face. "But the LORD said to him, 'Peace! Do not be afraid. You are not going to die.' So Gideon built an altar to the LORD there and called it The LORD is Peace" (vv. 23-24, *NIV*).

From this brief but life-changing encounter, Gideon, with a mere 300 men, defeated the Midianites, who were as "thick as locusts" (7:12). Gideon's weakness became his strength after his face-to-face encounter with God, and he was never the same. As a result of his sacrifice, Gideon discovered that God was his peace. Are you building an altar of experience that will change you?

Abraham's life-changing experience occurred at an altar as well. When Isaac, his promised son, was around 15 years old, God gave Abraham the most difficult test of his life. He instructed Abraham, "Take your son, your only son, Isaac, whom you love, and go to the region of Moriah. Sacrifice him there as a burnt offering on one of the mountains I will tell you about" (Gen. 22:2, *NIV*).

Abraham rose early the next morning and saddled the donkey with wood for the sacrifice. Abraham, Isaac and his two servants had walked for three days when Abraham looked up and saw the place in the distance. "He said to his servants, 'Stay here with the donkey while I and the boy go over there. We will worship and then we will come back to you'" (v. 5, *NIV*).

When Isaac asked his loving dad where the sacrificial lamb was, Abraham—brokenhearted yet faith-filled—explained that

God Himself would provide a lamb. Scripture records:

> When they reached the place God had told him about, Abraham built an altar there and arranged the wood on it. He bound his son Isaac and laid him on the altar, on top of the wood. Then he reached out his hand and took the knife to slay his son. But the angel of the LORD called out to him from heaven, "Abraham! Abraham!"
>
> "Here I am," [Abraham] replied.
>
> "Do not lay a hand on the boy," [the angel] said. "Do not do anything to him. Now I know that you fear God, because you have not withheld from me your son, your only son" (Gen. 22:9-12, *NIV*).

At that moment Abraham looked up and saw a ram caught in a thicket. He released Isaac, sacrificed the animal and worshiped God. Abraham named the altar "The Lord Will Provide" (Gen. 22:14). Just as the heavenly Father would one day sacrifice His Son, Jesus, for Abraham, He wanted to see if Abraham would sacrifice his son, Isaac, for Him. As a result of Abraham's obedience, he discovered that God was his provision.

My altar of experience changed my life forever, too. I named my altar "The Lord Is Present," for in it I learned that the world's best arguments and the opinions of men can never invalidate my experiences with the Lord! That early morning in 1970, as I surrendered my possessions, my dreams, my husband and children, and my ministry to the Lord, I was converted from living for myself to living for God's kingdom. As I relinquished everything in my control to Him, I was filled with His Holy Spirit.

An altar is a place of sacrifice and death, so beware of building an altar in an attempt to *get* something from God. You'll never be able to manipulate God toward your own ends. This isn't "let's make a deal." To sacrifice something to the Lord in order to receive something in return from Him is no sacrifice at all. God said that we are not to build an altar with dressed stones—human plans—and we are not to go up to our altar on steps—pride and self-promotion (see Exod. 20:24-26, *NIV*). Any true sacrifice will kill all self-interest. Sadly, most of us know sacrifice in theory, not in reality.

Have you built your altar? On that altar, were your eyes open to see God in a way you had never seen Him before? If not, then build an altar to Him today; climb upon it and ask for heaven's fire to consume you and for revelation to change you. I guarantee you will never be the same!

New Depths of Intimacy

If anyone thirsts, let him come to Me and drink. . . . As the Scripture has said, out of his heart will flow rivers of living water.

JOHN 7:37-38

In *Beyond the Veil*, I shared the following:

> Information will not transform you. Formulas will not bring you into intimacy with God. A lifestyle of intercession must be cultivated and maintained. Your inner man is like a garden and the disciplines of prayer keep it fertilized, watered, pruned and fruitful. Just as with any garden, time is needed for growth to appear. Seasons of difficulty and sunshine will be part of its lifelong development. But these seasons will force the roots deeper into the source of your strength—Jesus Christ. The following illustrates this principle:

> > A student asked the president of a school if he could take a shorter course than the one prescribed. "Oh yes," replied the president. "But then it depends upon what you want to be. When God wants to make an oak, He takes a hundred years. When He wants to make a squash, He takes only four months."

God wants you to be an oak tree, not a spiritual squash. To become an oak, your roots must sink down deep. If you are only willing to be a squash, your root system will remain shallow, and you will not have the vitality to linger very long in the Holy of Holies with God.[1]

Do you long to be closer to Jesus? The good news is that there is a way to develop a more intimate relationship with Him. The bad news is that this closeness will require time and effort on your part. It doesn't just happen—you must intentionally seek it.

When an old farm pump hasn't been used for a while, the farmer must prime it in order for it to be usable once again. He pours water into the shaft of the pump, displacing the air. Then, as the farmer thrusts the handle up and down, the suction created enables the pump to draw life-giving water from reservoirs deep below the surface of the earth. Soon fresh, clean water flows freely from the old pump's spout, satisfying any who are thirsty. To recapture or to establish your intimacy with Christ, it may be necessary for you to prime the pump.

You might begin to prime the pump with your love. Pour in love words and expressions of adoration. Express your love for the Lord with these words: "Father, you are so precious and I delight in you. Lord Jesus, you are everything to me. I need you more than I need my next breath. Holy Spirit, you are such a comfort to me. I appreciate the love, the joy and the peace you have brought into my life." As you prime the pump, doubt and indifference are displaced. Don't stop now! Keep repeating your love words. Allow them to reach deeply into your heart and to permeate your mind. Hesitate a moment so that your spirit can absorb these thoughts. James 4:8 tells us to "draw near to God and He will draw near to you." You are priming the pump by drawing near and loving Christ from your innermost being.

Soon the love of Christ will flood your heart and mind.

As time goes on, you will begin to notice that it requires less time on your part to prime the pump of your love. As you lose sight of self-interests and simply long for the interests of your Savior and Lord, ascending into His presence becomes almost effortless. Soon you will notice that the water—the living water—once so hard to draw to the surface, now flows freely, steadily, full and pure. As you continue to take the initiative in your intimate relationship with Jesus Christ in spirit-to-Spirit contact, the restlessness and anxiety you once knew will subside and fade into insignificance in the presence of the One you love.

Will you invest the time and effort necessary to begin to experience a new level of intimacy with Jesus? As you go through your day, speak love words to Jesus privately in your heart. Prime the pump and see love come alive!

Note
1. Alice Smith, *Beyond the Veil* (Ventura, CA: Regal Books, 1997), p. 69.

The DELIGHT

DELIGHT: A HIGH DEGREE OF GRATIFICATION;
SOMETHING THAT GIVES YOU GREAT PLEASURE;
THE POWER OF AFFORDING PLEASURABLE EMOTION.

---

*Nothing is more pleasant than to bask in God's glory.
Nothing is as glorious as being held in His strong
and loving spiritual embrace when He whispers the
secrets of His heart into yours. And there is no greater
delight than to see the smile on His adoring face
as you pray beyond the veil.*

Shepherd of Love

But when He saw the multitudes, He was moved with compassion for them, because they were weary and scattered, like sheep having no shepherd.

MATTHEW 9:36

One of my special girlfriends lives in Jerusalem. The threat of war, suicide bombings and unabated violence and hatred demand from her an extraordinary measure of faith in God. She shared this precious faith experience with me one day:

I have discovered a lot about myself. God has helped me through anger, shame, guilt and fear. As of today, I have received a major victory in each of these areas. I have a strange sense of God's peace and protection that I can't explain. I truly believe God has brought me to total trust and faith. This is something I have never had before. My life was controlled by feelings and not by faith. My past behavior was based on nothing *but* feelings. However, now I know a deep abiding faith that is based on trust.

This hasn't been an easy path but one of learning and adventure. I want to share an experience of a lady in my monthly prayer group. She lives on the border of Bethlehem, which has had some heavy fighting during the last several years. One night she looked out over the valley and heard gunfire and explosions. When she glanced down into the valley from her apartment window, she saw a shepherd calmly tending his sheep. With tears in her eyes, she said, "You could see he was talking to his sheep; and every time the gunfire would sound, the alarmed sheep would scatter." What happened next was the beginning of the life change for me.

My Israeli friend said that as the sheep scattered, the shepherd would simply take his staff and lightly touch each sheep and they would once again come into the fold. Our group began to weep. I read aloud from the 23rd Psalm, "Yea, though I walk through the valley of the shadow of death, I will fear no evil: for thou art with me; thy rod and thy staff they comfort me."

This is a beautiful picture of God's comforting peace during the storms of life. He is the Good Shepherd. He is the one who has promised to prepare a table before us in the presence of our enemies. Our loving Father is the one who has promised that He will never leave us nor forsake us. He is the shepherd who lays down His life for His sheep. What a consolation!

Interestingly, my friend's story took place in Bethlehem, where David, the shepherd boy, was quite familiar with sheep, since they were his trade. He later described the journey of Moses and the children of Israel with these words: "But He made His own people go forth like sheep, and guided them in the wilderness like a flock; and He led them on safely, so that they did not fear" (Ps. 78:52-53). Whatever you are facing today, you have no reason to fear, for your Good Shepherd will gently direct your path.

Every shepherd knows his sheep by name. Notice that when the sheep began to stray because of fear and distractions, the shepherd would tap them on their backs and no doubt speak their names, thus getting their attention. Once he diverted their attention from wandering, they would return to the fold. Believe it or not, even when we are fearful or distracted, Jesus is near to calm us with His gentle touch. If there is upheaval in your life today, it is proof positive that the Good Shepherd is gently handling your life; the Potter's tender hands are shaping you into the image of Christ! In *THE MESSAGE*, here is how Eugene Peterson translates Romans 8:29-30:

> God knew what he was doing from the very beginning. He decided from the outset to shape the lives of those who love him along the same lines as the life of his Son. The Son stands first in the line of humanity he restored. We see the original and intended shape of our lives there in him. After God made that decision of what his children should be like, he followed it up by calling people by name. After he called them by name, he set them on a solid basis with himself. And then, after getting them established, he stayed with them to the end, gloriously completing what he had begun.

The Lord is shepherding you today. Fears may rise up, discouragement may overtake your heart and trouble may cause you concern; but the Good Shepherd is always near to keep you close to the fold. Come close to Jesus right now, won't you?

Divine Intention

Let him kiss me with the kisses of his mouth—for your love is more delightful than wine. Pleasing is the fragrance of your perfumes; your name is like perfume poured out.
No wonder the maidens love you! Take me away with you—let us hurry! Let the king bring me into his chambers.

SONG OF SONGS 1:2-4, *NIV*

One day, years ago, I was in the mall with my children when I saw a young teenaged couple sitting on a bench making out. They were completely oblivious to the shoppers walking around them. People were so distracted by the couple's unusual behavior that they lost sight of what they were doing. All the while, I was trying to distract my young children, who were gawking at this inappropriate passionate behavior.

Lovers do not express their intimacy in public; they relate to one another in private. The same is true of our love relationship with the Lord Jesus. He has not chosen to relate to us as His business partner or His servant; He has taken us, for better or for worse, as His Bride. Jesus desires to commune intimately with us because He loves us and longs for fellowship with us. Don't answer the call of your Bridegroom from a sense of duty. Remarkably, His heart is filled with secrets that He wants to reveal to us. "The LORD confides in those who fear him; he makes his covenant known to them" (Ps. 25:14, *NIV*). What we receive in prayer, in our secret place with Jesus, the lover of our souls, we will live out in the everyday world. The love we feel in private will be manifest in the open in appropriate ways.

This close relationship the Lord longs to have with you is

not based on your worthiness. So resist the impulse to wait until you feel worthy to come to Him, because you never will be worthy of His wondrous love! It is a matter not of the mind but of the heart. For it is in your heart that God has placed His Spirit to bridge the chasm your sin created between you and your heavenly Groom.

Jesus, in wooing you, is destroying all your other lovers—the self being the biggest of them all. He is jealous for your total affection. A kiss is a very intimate transaction. Jesus wants to impart His love to you as He kisses you with favor, love and grace. Once you find yourself snuggled in the arms of your heavenly Bridegroom, you will be lifted out of self and centered in His purposes. Your heart will beat in sync with His. Your thoughts will be His thoughts and your desires will reflect His. You will have less concern for His meeting your needs and more concern for your meeting His needs.

Does God have needs? In one sense He does. Our self-limiting God has arranged the universe in such a way that He has chosen to be codependent on us. Jesus is looking for worshipers and intercessors. He has chosen to need us. And because He has, He will also equip us to fulfill His expectations with regard to this relationship. Amazing!

It is often said that the longer a married couple lives together, the more they look alike. The Father's plan is for us to grow into the likeness of Christ (see Rom. 8:29). In order for us to be conformed into His image, we must once and for all determine that we will not be conformed to the world (see Rom. 12:2). Your time spent in the prayer closet with Jesus will cause you to favor His likeness, and people will begin to see His glory reflected in you.

A vital relationship with your heavenly Groom is a partnership with a purpose. He desires to fill the earth with the knowledge of His glory (see Hab. 2:14). He does this by filling the earth

with sons and daughters born of His Spirit. As His bridal partner, we are critical to the fulfillment of the Great Commission.
He wants us, His Bride, to be pregnant with His burden for the
2.5 billion people who have never heard Calvary's love story.

Won't you seek your Bridegroom today in the bedchamber,
your prayer closet, so that Jesus' burden for the rest of the world
can be deposited in your heart? He is waiting for you now.

Struggling or Soaring?

*Being confident of this very thing, that He who has begun a
good work in you will complete it until the day
of Jesus Christ.*

PHILIPPIANS 1:6

Do you ever find yourself struggling in prayer? Are there days when it's easy to pray and other days when prayer appears to be next to impossible? Good—you're normal. But why does this happen?

During the years when Eddie and I were in evangelism, we traveled and lived in motor homes and travel trailers. When we were in our home on the road, we had our choice of two power sources. We could either draw electricity from the storage batteries, or we could generate electricity with our gasoline generator. Either of these sources would provide adequate lighting. However, the generator would actually provide AC power (just like in your home). We would have power enough to run our microwave, television, hair dryer or any other electrical appliance.

Like those trailers, inside of you there are two power sources for everything you do for God. You are either empowered by your soul—your mind, will and emotions—or your spirit—that place in you where God lives. In fact, one or the other will also generate your prayers. Your prayers are either soulish or spiritual. It's sometimes hard to distinguish between the two. But like our gasoline-powered generator compared with the storage batteries, spirit-generated prayer will be far more effective than soul-centered praying. This, then, is the source of your struggle.

When you're struggling in prayer, it is likely that you're praying soulishly. You are praying out of your humanity rather than out of your divinity. The apostle Peter wrote, "God made great and marvelous promises, so that *his nature would become part of us.* Then we could escape our evil desires and the corrupt influences of this world" (2 Pet. 1:4, *CEV*, emphasis added). This struggle is actually good in some ways. It enables you to see the distinction between when the soul is *forcing* your prayer and when the Holy Spirit is *directing* your prayer (see Rom. 8:26).

First Corinthians 6:17 in the *Contemporary English Version* says, "But anyone who is joined to the Lord is *one in spirit* with him" (emphasis added). So anyone who has been born again has the Spirit of Christ. John the beloved, Jesus' most intimate disciple, wrote, "God has given us *his Spirit.* That is how we know that we are *one with him,* just as *he is one with us*" (1 John 4:13, *CEV*, emphasis added). When the Spirit of God, who lives in your spirit, is guiding your prayer, it is as if your prayer life is being lifted up in a hot air balloon. The heat generated by your passion for Christ causes the balloon of your prayer life to rise. It rises above your anxiety, your doubt and your distractions. As it rises, the wind of the Holy Spirit begins to propel it forward into the things that are on the heart of the Father. As the balloon glides through the sky, you can sit back and enjoy the ride.

Eventually, as the temperature in the balloon begins to drop, you begin to lose altitude. What are you to do? No problem. The air in the balloon must be reheated. As you turn your heart's focus once again from your own thoughts, your own requests and your own desires and once again revel in who He is to you, your passion is rekindled and the temperature rises. As it does, your balloon ascends to new and more glorious heights.

This is how you maintain intimacy with Jesus. Struggling or striving to love the Lord or to perform doesn't renew your love. Focusing your thoughts on the Lord Jesus, His promises, His person and who He is to you does! As you brag on Him and thank Him for who He is and what He has done for you; as you remind Him of His promises and praise Him for His faithfulness, the Holy Spirit stokes the fire in your heart and stirs up your passion for Him.

You no longer self-consciously struggle against your own thoughts, feelings and will. You are not even conscious of your surroundings. Now you are soaring above Earth's atmosphere in the heavenlies. You are not lost in space, but you are lost in His presence! You ascend from this earth and soar to unexplored heights reserved for those who diligently seek Him. And when you reach "cruising altitude," the wind of the Spirit of God begins to guide you again into what is on the Father's heart.

An unbroken person will never have the faith necessary to submit to the Spirit of God. Without brokenness, we remain independent and see things from the outside in, resisting any work from the inside out. Unable to yield to the process of brokenness and driven to guard our own hearts and protect our domain, we will sadly remain earthbound.

Aren't you hungry today for a fresh, intimate encounter with the Lord? Guess what? Believe it or not, you are not as hungry for Him as He is for a fresh, intimate encounter with you. He actually longs for you! Psalm 25:14 says, "God-friendship is for God-worshipers; they are the ones he confides in" (*THE MESSAGE*). Think of it! There are secrets on the Father's heart today that He longs to share with you.

Saving Grace

The blood of Jesus Christ His Son cleanses us from all sin.

1 JOHN 1:7

A coal miner once said to a preacher, "You know, I'd like to be a Christian, but I can't believe in what you said tonight."

"Why not?" asked the preacher.

"Well, I'd give anything to believe that God would forgive my sins, but I can't believe that He'll forgive me if all I do is turn to Him. It's too cheap."

"Did you work in the mine today?" the preacher asked.

Surprised, the man replied, "Yes, I was down in the pit as usual. Why?"

"How did you get out of the pit?"

"The way I usually do. I got into the cage and was pulled to the top."

"How much did you pay to be pulled out of the pit?"

The miner looked at the preacher in astonishment. "Pay? Of course I didn't pay anything."

"Well," said the preacher, "weren't you afraid to trust your life to that cage? Wasn't it too cheap?"

"Oh, no! It was cheap for *me,* but it cost the company a lot of money to sink that shaft and buy that equipment." Then the implication of what he had said struck him, and he saw that though God offered him salvation without price, it wasn't cheap at all. In fact, it had cost God a great price to rescue lost men: the blood of His sinless Son!

Can you see it? Look at the blood of Jesus. Gory? Yes. But

also *glory*! His precious blood is the price God was willing to pay for you and for me. His precious blood was not the blood of mortal men. We're talking about the blood of almighty God! In it was no generational iniquity or taint of sin. Not one lie, misspoken word or misdeed. This was sinless blood! And even greater, in this perfect blood is the power to redeem and to reconcile any person to God.

An American missionary who was trying to translate the Bible into an African dialect came to the word "redeem." *What word in this tribal language could possibly be synonymous?* he wondered. When he asked one of the natives, the man smiled and suggested a word in his language that the missionary promptly used in his Bible translation: the word for "he took my neck out."

Hundreds of years earlier, when slave traders had rounded up people to take back to the new world, they would put iron stocks around the natives' necks. The stocks were then chained together. When the chain gang came through a village on the way to the slave ship, if someone saw a friend or relative held captive and was able to pay, the slave's neck was removed from the iron stock and the person was allowed to leave the chain gang. Their redemption came as they "took their neck out" of the chains of bondage!

That is what Jesus' blood has done for us. It has *freed* us! And not only has the blood taken our necks out, but it also *reconciles* our record with God. "Reconcile" is a financial term that refers to balancing an account. Jesus' blood has eradicated the errors, the sins, on our account. His blood has provided our atonement. I have heard it said that atonement means at-one-ment with God! Though our sins are as scarlet, His blood keeps on cleansing us from sin. There is not a spot left! We are accepted in the Beloved!

Finally, the blood of Jesus *preserves* us. Just as the blood sprinkled on the doorposts of the Israelites' homes protected them from the destroying angel, Jesus' blood protects us from the destruction that Satan would desire for us. John wrote, "They overcame him by the blood of the Lamb" (Rev. 12:11). Can anyone or anything be victorious over the blood of Christ? The blood alone cleanses, revives, preserves and keeps us! As the old hymn says, "O precious is the flow that makes me white as snow; no other fount I know, nothing but the blood of Jesus!"[1]

Note

1. Robert Lowry, "Nothing but the Blood," quoted in *The Celebration Hymnal* (n.p.: Word Music/Integrity Music, 1997), song 337.

Shower Him with Spiritual Gifts

～

*Let us continually offer to God a sacrifice of praise—
the fruit of lips that confess his name.*

HEBREWS 13:15, *NIV*

For most of us, the words "spiritual gifts" bring to mind God's gifts to us by the Holy Spirit—the gifts of teaching, giving and exhortation as well as the other four motivational gifts listed in Romans 12; the gifts of prophecy, miracles, tongues and the other six manifestation gifts listed in 1 Corinthians 12; the gifts of apostle, prophet, pastor-teacher and evangelist listed in Ephesians 4.

Not only does God give us supernatural spiritual gifts, but He also gives us every physical gift: "Every good gift and every perfect gift is from above, and comes down from the Father of lights, with whom there is no variation or shadow of turning" (Jas. 1:17). Health, food, clothing, family, friends, money and more are all expressions of grace from our favorful and faithful Father. God continually showers us with gifts—both inward and outward!

It isn't difficult to think how we can give back physical gifts to God—our time, tithes and offerings are good examples of that. But did you ever stop to think that we can also give a spiritual gift to God? Can you think of one spiritual gift we should continually shower on Him? You probably know where I'm headed now. I'm talking about an attitude of gratitude (see 1 Thess. 5:18). Unfortunately, if there is one grievous and besetting sin in America today, it is the sin of ingratitude. As I travel the nations, the places where God seems to be doing the most are among people who are utterly and outspokenly grateful to Him for even the smallest blessings. This—a heart filled with gratitude and praise for who He is—is the spiritual gift He desires us to shower on Him!

A wife asked her husband of many years if he loved her. He told her that of course he did. To this she said, "Then why don't you ever tell me?" Dryly, he replied, "Honey, I told you 'I love you' when I married you. If I ever change my mind, I'll let you know."

We often live like this clueless husband—forgetting that the greatest spiritual gift we can give to God is our love (see 1 Cor. 13:13). To love Him means to focus our attention on Him and shower Him with our affection. Focusing our attention means that we merge His person and His will into every experience and aspect of our lives and our thinking. Because God does not change (see Mal. 3:6), if there is something we are doing or thinking that cannot be merged naturally with who He is, then we need to change.

We cannot continue to think and do what conflicts with who He is and who we are in Him. To do so will make us unstable, and instability in even one area of our lives will make us unstable in all our ways! James 1:8 tells us that a double-minded person is "unstable in all his ways." Loving God means that we focus on Him and incorporate Him into our lives so that we live totally for Him. We honor God this way.

If we cherish the Lord, we will tell Him so. Don't make God your mind reader; He has ears! Just as He hears the prayers of His people, He also hears their praise. Only a God with ears would make birds that sing, puppies that yap and donkeys that bray, and having done so brag, "This is good!"

God created you with the ability to verbalize and orally declare His goodness, grace and mercy. So speak your heart to Him.

But can't He read my mind? you ask. *Doesn't He know what I feel even before I feel it? Then what's the point of saying it?*

The Father not only loves to hear the melodic tones of the sparrow, but His heart also hangs on every word of love and praise you speak. It is like honey to His heart. The angels surrounding His throne must surely envy the look that appears on His face when He hears you say, "Thank You, Lord, for saving my soul." With all the praise the angels can muster—and they offer Him praise day and night—that simple sentence of gratitude is one they cannot express and will never experience!

Another reason for speaking your praise aloud to God is that you need to say it. Matthew 12:34 says, "For out of the abundance of the heart the mouth speaks." Your heart and mouth are inextricably attached. They reveal each other. You are being transformed by the words you say. If you constantly confess the negative, then your heart will become more negative. As you constantly hear yourself praise and thank Him aloud, your heart is changed (see Rom. 10:17)!

Another reason to praise God out loud is to declare His victory to the whole spiritual world. From the day we were born, we have been and will continue to be constantly monitored by both God and the enemy. Praising God aloud declares His goodness into the air where the enemy, the prince of the power of the air, can hear it (see Eph. 2:2). God has destined us, His Bride, to do this (see Eph. 3:10).

Yes, we have a heavenly Father who continually showers us with all good things. But does He have children who think about what they can give to Him? What spiritual gifts are you offering to the Lord today? Even if you haven't a dime, the one gift you can consistently and continually shower on Him is the one gift He most longs to receive—a grateful heart of praise!

Heart to Heart

Surely the Lord GOD does nothing, unless He reveals His secret to His servants.

AMOS 3:7, NKJV

My friend Kay Arthur, founder of Precept Ministries, tells the following story that wonderfully illustrates how perseverance works to bring us to a place of intimacy in prayer:

> My husband Jack and I were watching a medical program on television one night. They showed an open-heart surgery. Two human hearts were lying side by side. Each was beating at different rhythms. The surgeon moved them together, until the tissue of one heart touched the other. Suddenly, both assumed the same rhythm.[1]

This is an amazing picture of intimacy. As our hearts touch the Father's heart, we assume the same rhythm, the same desires and the same goals. The more we know Him, the more we love Him. Hopelessly in love with Him, our goals are lost in His.[2]

His burden becomes the focus of our intercession. We begin to see issues as He sees them. Our hearts become united with His. The hungering heart that burns with desire for intimate communion will be enabled by the Holy Spirit to taste the joys of heaven and experience the ecstasy of seeing many people prayed into the kingdom of God.[3]

Jesus' powerful ministry rested on one important factor: He had power for ministry because His heart literally beat as one with His heavenly Father's heart. He lived in total intimacy with the Father. This was revealed when Jesus said, "I tell you the truth, the Son can do nothing by himself [powerlessness]; he can do only what he sees his Father doing, because whatever the Father does the Son also does [powerful]" (John 5:19, *NIV*).

God's divine purposes will be revealed to you as your heart touches His and begins to beat in rhythm with His. From this new level of relationship, you will move from problem-centered prayer to purpose-driven prayer. Problem-centered prayer is focused on our needs. Often we complain in prayer about a situation that needs a change. Purpose-driven prayer focuses on God's overarching plan. By faith you can pray for His maximum glory to be achieved in any situation. This frees the Lord to replace your problem with His provision!

Powerlessness largely results from prayerlessness, and prayerlessness is a result of our failure to grasp the purposes of God through intimate communion with Him. We are eating the fruit of prayerlessness, and our children, government, churches and society are reaping the result of dry eyes in the pews and crusty hearts in the pulpits.[4]

Instead of pursuing intimacy with the Father, many Christians are infatuated with warfare, convinced that time in prayer is best spent addressing the enemy. Their prayer life is out of balance. If you want to know the Father's secrets and experience the Father's anointing, then make the necessary investment before His throne to receive these things. Remember, your authority over the enemy will never exceed your intimacy with the Father.

The ultimate Christian experience is intimate union with God—your heart beating in sync with His. Not only does this experience satisfy your need for relationship, but it also compels you to pray for His kingdom to come on Earth as it is in heaven. Many Christians are lonely, empty people who search for completeness. Are you lonely today? Enter the throne room, give your heart to Jesus, and your loneliness will dissipate in His presence. Then join Him by standing in the gap for souls who are more than lonely—they are lost!

Amazingly, the Father longs for intimacy with you more than you long for intimacy with Him. Perhaps this is because He alone fully knows what is at stake—billions of souls who have yet to hear His message of salvation!

Have you been viewing the Great Commission as a human evangelistic enterprise rather than the result of an intimate partnership with the Most High God? Are you wallowing in the despair of problem-centered prayer? Get the big picture! The final fruit of your partnership with Christ in purpose-driven prayer is the completion of the Great Commission. Aren't you ready to connect with what is on His heart today? Then enlarge your vision, get in sync with His heart and claim the victory for your life, your family and your nation.

Notes
1. Kay Arthur, quoted in Alice Smith, *Beyond the Veil* (Ventura, CA: Regal Books, 1997), p. 23.
2. Alice Smith, *Beyond the Veil* (Ventura, CA: Regal Books, 1997), p. 23.
3. Ibid.
4. Ibid., p. 17.

The Holy of Holies

How lovely is your dwelling place, O LORD Almighty! My soul yearns, even faints, for the courts of the LORD; my heart and my flesh cry out for the living God.

PSALM 84:1-2

Two thousand years ago Jesus hung on the cross and cried out, "It is finished!" At the sound of those words, the flesh over His heart ripped in two, redeeming fallen humanity from eternal separation with God. Heaven's windows opened and the hand of God reached into the temple tearing the veil in the Holy of Holies from top to bottom. God's heart was forever exposed to all who would seek Him. His heart was open to all who would commune with Him. His throne room was now accessible to all who would enter.

"It is finished!" Finished forever are the days when God is unapproachable; finished forever are the days when His children must stand outside as the high priest intercedes for them. God Himself initiated the level of intimate intercession that can occur only beyond the veil. Such communion with God is prayer at its deepest level. And it is available to all who will come into the "the inner chamber" of the Holy of Holies.[1]

The angels know the dimensions of your dynamic relationship with the Lord. They have seen the yearning of God's heart reflected in His face—a yearning simply to be with you. Heaven's hosts applaud with delight as you enter through the door into the Lord's inner chamber, the Holy of Holies, and are enveloped by the sheer radiance of His glory!

It is difficult for us to imagine how in Old Testament times only one man, the high priest, could enter the Holy of Holies; and he could only enter once each year. Because he was the only qualified priest, the other priests would live their entire lives without ever having the opportunity to enter the Holy of Holies. And women? Forget it. It was a man thing. Now look at you! Peter says you are a chosen generation and a royal priesthood (see 1 Pet. 2:9). As a priest of God, you are a guest invited beyond the veil. It doesn't matter if you are a woman or a man; you can enter joyfully and boldly at any time because of the blood of Jesus Christ shed on Calvary (see Heb. 10:19-20).

Draw near with sincerity into the Holy of Holies with your heart full of faith as you wait expectantly for the Lord Himself to appear to you. You are positioning yourself for what others say is impossible: an audience with the Most High God! And sure enough He arrives. As He enters your prayer room, His train fills the temple. His glory cloud surrounds you and His presence mesmerizes. Almighty God is the center of it all—He is the glorious one! You begin to bow when suddenly and inexplicably you fall on your face before Him. This is the most sacred spot on Earth—or is this Earth? Are you not caught up in His presence, lost in His glory? Earth has lost all significance to you now.

Intercession is a stethoscope to the heart of God. *Shhh!* Listen! The more you listen, the more you'll hear His heart. The more you hear His heart, the more transformed into His likeness you will become. Can you hear it even now? That is the Father's heartbeat. Listen carefully. You'll soon discover that His heart beats for your company.

Jesus invites you to a table set for two: "Here I am! I stand at the door and knock. If anyone hears my voice and opens the door, I will come in and eat with him, and he with me" (Rev. 3:20, *NIV*). He said that if you will open the door and invite Him in, He will sit down and sup with you. At this table for two the Spirit of God prepares and serves the spiritual cuisine Christ offers you. The diet is varied. One day it may be a revelation, the next day it may be a reassurance. Another day the Lord may promise you an answer to prayer. Our nourishment comes not only from His love words, but it also comes from being in His presence. It is good that you have entered with an appetite for the Lord!

One of the keys to knowing Christ in the intimate Holy of Holies is to lay down your preconceptions. You will never fully understand heavenly protocol, so check all expectations at the door. After all, self is not allowed into this level of intimate intercession. This is no place for self-centered childishness. This is no time to force your requests upon Him or take advantage of His attention with your gripes or greed. This Spirit-to-spirit communion will dissipate at the slightest evidence of self-domination.

Although the door of intimacy is open to all who will enter, few actually take advantage of this rich place of prayer. The Lord delights in the believer who yearns to know what cannot be known except through pressing in beyond the torn veil into His holy presence. Won't you come close to Him now? He's sitting at the table for two, waiting for you!

Note
1. Alice Smith, *Beyond the Veil* (Ventura, CA: Regal Books, 1997), p. 167.

Where Is My Bride?

For your Maker is your husband—the LORD Almighty is His name.

There are few things more memorable than a wedding. As the beautifully decorated church fills with people, the bride and bridegroom make last-minute preparations for the momentous event. Finally the moment is here. After months of preparation, the wedding begins. Accompanied by music, the bridesmaids and groomsmen walk down the aisle and take their places. Next, the pastor and the groom enter. The guests smile with approval at how handsome and proud the groom looks. Now everyone is poised to see one person—the bride.

The wedding march begins, and as the music swells, the doors swing open and there she is in all her beauty, dressed in pure white. Her gorgeous gown flows gracefully as she makes her way down the aisle toward her groom. Everything about her is perfect: her hair, her nails, her makeup. The audience stands in honor of her and turns to look. Admiring whispers can be heard as she is escorted to the front. At the altar the bride and groom face the pastor and the ceremony begins.

A new covenant—a new beginning! Two become one. The invited guests listen with delight as the happy couple pledge themselves to each other and promise God that they will honor this commitment forever!

This is the start of a great new life. But it's only the start. Everyone knows that the end of the ceremony is only the beginning of the marriage. The marriage bond is actually consummated behind closed doors, in a private place. There the bride gives herself freely and intimately to this man she loves.

The wedding scene I have just described is analogous to our intimate journey with the Lord Jesus. At salvation, we were wed to Him. We are His Bride and He is waiting for us to come to Him. Paul used the same image when he said, "I am jealous for you, just as God is; you are like a pure virgin whom I have promised in marriage to one man only, Christ himself" (2 Cor. 11:2, *TEV*). God is our Bridegroom, and today He is asking, "Where is My Bride? Why doesn't she come into the quiet place of prayer and spend time with Me?"

Christ is the only groom I know whose bride will hardly speak to Him. We often appear to be more interested in other things, yet we wonder why our churches are empty, our ministries powerless and our altars barren. It is because we are giving ourselves to other lovers! Hear the burden of God's heart: "I remember the devotion of your youth, how as a bride you loved me and followed me through the desert, through a land not sown" (Jer. 2:2, *NIV*). Yet Israel didn't want to be faithful to God. The Lord was grieved. "Long ago you broke off your yoke and tore off your bonds; you said: 'I will not serve you!' Indeed, on every high hill and under every spreading tree you lay down as a prostitute" (Jer. 2:20, *NIV*).

The indictment is far worse for New Covenant people. In the Old Testament the people of God didn't have the Holy Spirit living in them as we do. The Lord is crying, "Where is My Bride?" We might be busy with home, career, children or making money. Doing church can even become a god. We can be more in love with the work of the Lord than with the Lord of the work. We, His Bride, have lifted our skirt under every spreading tree to commit adultery with the world. We have given our hearts to the idolatry of houses, cars, children, amusement and money. These have captured our attention from our heavenly Groom.

Perhaps you have been so caught up in the world and the affairs of life that you have all but forgotten your Bridegroom. Stop right now and gently whisper your apology to Him. Ask your heavenly Groom to forgive you for being attracted to and distracted by other things. If you are thinking, *I didn't know I was unfaithful to Jesus, but right now I want to renew my wedding vows,* then write your name in the blanks below. Slowly and deliberately read aloud your vow to Jesus. Once you have done this, read aloud what the Lord Jesus, your Groom, pledges to you.

I, _____ , take You, Jesus, to be my lawfully wedded husband, to have and to hold from this day forward. I pledge before God and these witnesses [heavenly witnesses] to be Your loving and faithful Bride. I will love and honor You, cherish and obey You, and forsaking all others, I will keep myself totally for You, Jesus. In plenty and in want, in joy and in sorrow, in sickness and in health, through adversity or suffering, I will trust You. I give my whole heart to You, Lord, in token and pledge of my constant faith and abiding love.

I, Jesus, take you, _____ , to be My chosen wedded Bride, to have and to hold you from eternity past, and forever. I have formed you and called you out of darkness. I bought you with My life, and I have fulfilled the law for you. I am preparing a place for you, that where I am, you may be also. I will never leave you or forsake you. Call unto Me and I will answer you. I will always be a shield about you. I have given you My name

and all authority to use it. You are My beloved. My blood
I give for you, in token and pledge of My constant devotion to you.

It bears repeating: You are Husband and wife! Now enjoy the
love of your life!

THE DEVOTION

DEVOTION: ARDENT, OFTEN SELFLESS AFFECTION AND
DEDICATION, AS TO A PERSON.

*Devotion to God—found in the purity, faithfulness
and perseverance of prayer—prepares us for
understanding His ways. Our journey beyond the veil
leads us to know Him and to delight in living for
Him. In His holy presence we cannot help but fall
in love with Him over and over again!*

Tenacity in Prayer

*Then He spoke a parable to them, that men always
ought to pray and not lose heart.*

LUKE 18:1

I grew up along the Gulf Coast of Texas and have always loved
to fish. So several years ago, when our family went on vacation
to Puerto Vallerta, Mexico, one of my expectations was to go
deep-sea fishing. Eddie arranged the deal with two Hispanic
men on their well-equipped private boat.

The next morning, *very* early, we arrived at the boat dock. As
we stepped onto the boat, Eddie pointed out to me how expen-
sive the rods and reels were. Since we would be fishing for sailfish and marlin, the rigs we used cost from $800 to $1,000 each.
I was so nervous about losing the rig that my knuckles turned
white as I held on tightly to the rod.

Soon, however, the boat ride began to relax me. With the
rhythm of the boat over the waves, I started to get sleepy. Twenty
minutes later we arrived at just the right spot to fish. The captain told us we needed live bait, so Eddie accommodated us
immediately by catching a small tuna—perfect bait for big fish.

Two hours passed. We had paid for four hours, and now half
of our time was gone. Except for Eddie's six-inch tuna, we had
caught nothing. I was beginning to worry. So I decided to pray.
Jesus tells us to pray about everything, and I really wanted to
catch a trophy-sized fish. I told the captain and his friend that I
was going to pray to Jesus that I would catch a big fish. He and
his shipmate looked at me with disbelief. Hey, the world desper-

ately needs to see nonreligious attitudes among Christians, so I began to speak with my eyes open and said, "Lord Jesus, You own all the fish in this huge ocean. I am asking You right now to let me catch a very big one. Thank You for hearing my prayer. Amen." It was humorous, because the men had removed their caps and bowed their heads. At the end of my prayer, they repeated "amen" after me.

Less than three minutes later, a gorgeous sailfish leaped out of the water. His snout was long and slender, his fins fully extended. The beautiful blue fish struggled to free himself from my line. I was ecstatic! This sailfish was on my line, and now I was in the fight to bring him in.

Neither Eddie nor the men helped me with the line, but they carefully instructed me on how to reel in the fish. As soon as I engaged the fish in the fight, other party boats began to circle ours. I could almost feel the spite of the professional fishermen as they watched me from afar. (Smile.)

I screamed almost the entire 35 minutes it to took to tire the fish! The strength of that sailfish was tremendous—indescribable. Two times I reeled the fish to the boat only to have it gain new energy and run. It was so difficult to release the line and allow the fish to run, for I knew it was going to require more tenacity and determination on my part to reel him in again. But I was determined to win the battle and land this fish. Finally, the fish tired. The third time I pulled the fish near the boat, it was too exhausted to resist. The fish was mine! We pulled this eight-foot, one-inch beauty into the boat—all 80 pounds of it! Perhaps you're wondering why I'm telling you this fish story. Is it because I want to brag a little? Well, maybe. But there is another reason.

While I struggled with my line, I had seriously questioned my ability to catch the fish. Doubt flooded my mind. I was tired and thirsty. My arms ached. The strength of the fish was intense. People all around me were watching to see if I would stick with the fight. Although I had prayed to Jesus for this blessing, now my faith was being tested.

Intercessory prayer is not unlike what I went through to catch that sailfish. God gives us a burden. The load is heavy and the struggle is intense. It may be about your wayward child. Just like that fish, one minute your child appears to be repenting and then off he or she runs. You pray even more. You ask the Lord to answer your prayer, and He puts you in the fight of your life. Jesus told us, "And from the days of John the Baptist until now the kingdom of heaven suffers violence, and the violent take it by force" (Matt. 11:12).

Effective, prevailing prayer can require extreme effort. It is a fight—a spiritual violence that has you hanging on to the promises of God with white-knuckled intensity. Your child is running from God and doesn't want anything to do with Him. Just hang on to the rig! Don't let go. You might even see a small breakthrough; but until your child is in the boat of salvation and victory, you must remain engaged in the battle. It requires tenacity, determination, faith and confidence in God and His Word to get the big fish into the boat.

This story applies to someone you know—a friend, a husband, a child, a parent. Keep fishing. Don't give up! Pray! Hang on to God's promises, and someday you will land the big one!

Purity

Blessed are the pure in heart, for they shall see God.

MATTHEW 5:8

$\mathcal{I}$ have been to Israel several times, and one of my favorite things to do is to view the city model of Old Testament Jerusalem to see what the Temple might have looked like in Solomon's day. The Old Testament Temple must have been magnificent: "Across the front of the temple was a porch thirty feet wide and thirty feet high. The inside walls of the porch were covered with pure gold. Solomon had the inside walls of the temple's main room paneled first with pine and then with a layer of gold, and he had them decorated with carvings of palm trees and designs that looked like chains. Two columns were made for the entrance to the temple. Each one was fifty-two feet tall and had a cap on top that was seven and a half feet high" (2 Chron. 3:4-5,15, *CEV*). No building could compare!

Allow me to paint a mental image for you. Inside this gorgeous ornate Temple, the first layer of the walls and ceiling was fir wood overlaid with pure gold. (The wood is symbolic of our humanity, and the pure gold is symbolic of the divine work of Christ in us.) Images of cherubim were engraved on its golden walls. The Bible says that the Temple was beautifully adorned with precious stones. Solomon's Temple was one of the wonders of the then-known world.

One day, as I was thinking and praying about the Temple, the Father said to me: "Alice, as I overlaid the inside of the Temple with pure gold, so am I doing inside of you. I am purifying your

Temple and overlaying it with pure gold."

The Lord has done this work in me in many ways through the years, but one particular instance comes to mind. In 1972, Eddie and I were part of a genuine revival of repentance and salvation. We were the evangelistic singers for the meetings when the move of God began. All night long, night after night at the church, people would lay on the floor groaning and crying out to the Lord. It looked like a battle zone of slain soldiers throughout the auditorium.

For hours on end, people wept in repentance for even the smallest sins. A fifth-grade boy stood before the congregation and wept as though he had committed a grave sin in stealing cookies from the church kitchen. One wealthy woman confessed that she had kept for herself the perfect-attendance pins the girls in her Sunday School class had earned. The conviction of God was palpable. I couldn't sleep; I couldn't eat. I felt miserable as the Lord revealed my selfish and soulish immaturity. One night, instead of preparing for the service (at which we were the guest singers), I decided to stay in the hotel room. However, Eddie confronted me and my rebellion. I pouted and complained but went to the service anyway. That evening the Spirit of the Lord touched me in a significant way. When I stood up again after a time of praying on the floor, a fresh wave of His holiness and purity had been revealed to me.

God's preferred method for purifying our lives is to test our faith. Peter says, "In this you greatly rejoice, though now for a little while you may have had to suffer grief in all kinds of trials. These have come so that your faith—of greater worth than gold, which perishes even though refined by fire—may be proved genuine and may result in praise, glory and honor when Jesus Christ is revealed" (1 Pet. 1:6-7, *NIV*).

As Eddie and I mentioned in our book *The Advocates,* jewelers work with different purities of gold:

There is gold-plated, gold-filled, 10K, 14K, 18K and 24K gold. Master designers will tell you that the purer the gold, the softer it is. The same is true in our lives—the trials of our lives, like a refiner's fire, burn away impurities. As a result, a softening takes place in our lives that makes us pliable and more easily conformed into the image of Christ (see Rom. 8:29).[1]

Purity is meaningless until it is tested. We will know that we have passed a test of purity when we no longer say, "Do I really have to give that up, too?" Even asking the question suggests that we have not settled in our hearts to live solely for Christ. Once all questions are gone and our determination is sure, then the process of purity has begun to work in us. God used the loss of three babies, the loss of every earthly possession except for the clothes on our backs and the suffering of betrayal more than once to test and purify our hearts. If you will let Him, He will use the experiences of your life to purify you. What you live through will always make you either bitter or better—the choice is yours.

Purity, integrity and impeccable character are prerequisites for effective ministry and are forged in God's furnace and birthed out of death to self. These character qualities are essentially manifestations of Christ's living in us. So the tests the Father puts us through draw attention to our faults. It is during the testing that we, and those around us, discover what we are really like.

David the psalmist posed the question:

Who may ascend into the hill of the LORD? Or who may stand in His holy place? He who has clean hands and a pure heart, who has not lifted up his soul to an idol, nor sworn deceitfully. He shall receive blessing from the LORD, and righteousness from the God of his salvation (Ps. 24:3-5).

We shouldn't be surprised then that after David became king and committed his notorious sin with Bathsheba, he would pray, "Create in me a clean [pure] heart, O God, and renew a steadfast spirit within me" (Ps. 51:10).

Purity for the intercessor requires continual exposure to Jesus' presence. I call it transformation by adoration. The Lord Jesus is in the process of overlaying your temple with gold. Go to Him today with your flaws, your faults and your failures. He who loves you unconditionally will bring you to conviction, repentance and cleansing as you submit yourself to Him in voluntary devotion. Once purified, you can say with David, "Then I will teach transgressors Your ways, and sinners shall be converted to You" (Ps. 51:13).

Note

1. Eddie and Alice Smith, *The Advocates: How to Plead the Case of Others in Prayer* (Lake Mary, FL: Charisma Books, 2001), p. 6.

A Living Canvas

Choose for yourselves this day whom you will serve.

JOSHUA 24:15

On the ground of our own goodness we cannot expect to have our prayers answered. But Jesus is worthy, and for His sake we may have our prayers answered. . . . And if we trust in [Christ], if we hide in Him, if we put Him forward and ourselves in the background, depend on Him and plead His name, we may expect to have our prayers answered.

GEORGE MÜLLER

The eternal life within us is God's own life. He is the Eternal. The life that I now share with Him came from Him. He is its source, its course (direction) and its force (power). My spiritual life is as dependent on Him as my physical life is dependent on the air I breathe. My spiritual life is sustained by my constant, faithful communion with God. Israel discovered that yesterday's manna was tasteless. I have discovered that yesterday's communion with the Father will not suffice for today. I must faithfully attend to the care and feeding of my spiritual condition. I must stay in constant touch with heaven. This is an expression of my *faithfulness to God*.

My *devotion to God* is demonstrated by my inclusion of Him in my daily schedule. As I set aside time to draw apart from my busyness and the world's distractions and to quiet myself before Him, I express to Him His value to me. I acknowledge who He is and who He is to me, what He's done throughout history and what He's done for me, what He is doing in the earth today and what He is doing in my life today. Our God is attracted to acknowledgment and gratitude. He relishes it!

God *is*. And God rewards those who diligently seek Him! The old hymn rightly says that it takes time to be holy.

It's strange to me that we even have to address this issue. For we are nothing without Him—altogether undone. We are doomed without the blood of Christ and damned without the life of Christ. How can we not take time each day to bow before Him humbly and gratefully? How can we not draw near to Him when He has told us that He will draw near to us when we draw near to Him (see Jas. 4:8)? How can we not run to Him and access the wealth of His riches that He has already bountifully bestowed upon us (see Eph. 1:1-14)!

But there is more than our faithfulness *to* God to consider. There is also our faithfulness *for* God. Just as we "willed" to receive Christ, so must we "will" to walk in Him. No one drifts into being faithful. Faithfulness is a matter of choice. It is a calculated move. We are to be "outworking" what He is "inworking" in us. Just as Jesus became flesh and dwelt among men, we are to allow Him to become flesh today—in us! God wants you and me to be conformed to the image of His Son so that others can see our good works and glorify Him. God's glory is the fruit of faithfulness!

We faithfully reflect Christ on two levels. The first level is in *the likeness of His death*. We must die to sin and to the pull of this world. We must die to our own plans and desires. Paul said that he died daily (see 1 Cor. 15:31).

The second level is that we are to display the Lord in *the power of His resurrection*. We do this by faithfully refusing sin and living a fully surrendered life to God. And as we do, the power of His death and resurrection works in us through His Holy Spirit.

Eddie, my husband, was a 19-year-old sailor in the United States Navy when he was stationed aboard the U.S.S. *McCormick*

(DDG-8), a guided-missile destroyer, in the Pacific. When he came aboard, he was ridiculed because he didn't curse, drink, smoke or womanize as the others did. His commitment to Christ and Christ's presence in his life made some feel uncomfortable in their sin.

But as the months passed and sin began to take its toll on their lives, these same men would secretly come to Eddie for counseling. One man who had scoffed at him for not taking advantage of the illicit sex in the foreign ports was now going home to his wife with a sexually transmitted disease.

Christ in Eddie kept him from sin. Christ through Eddie brought comfort, counsel and salvation to others.

Our lives are a living canvas on which the Holy Spirit is painting God's message of love for the world. He wants the world to see those works of art, so they can respond to Him as you and I once did. That can only happen if we are truly faithful to Him—not just at special times, but continually. For there is no sacred and secular in the life of a true believer. *Everything about your life is sacred!*

George Müller prayed for 52 years for the son of his best friend to come to Christ. It was at Müller's funeral, as his casket was being lowered into the ground, that the son gave his heart and life to Jesus Christ. A life redeemed because of one man's faithfulness and, I'm sure, the beauty of Jesus' life clearly displayed in him!

The fact that you are reading these words tells me that you have made your choice to forsake yesterday's manna and feed on today's Bread of Life! Will you also choose to represent the Father faithfully today so that others may see a clear picture of who He is in you?

Listening

〜

*He will fulfill the desire of those that fear him; He also
will hear their cry and save them.*

PSALM 145:19

All my life I have been a talker. I love to talk! Good thing I
became a preacher. I remember how in school I would get excited
about something going on in the class and turn to my classmate
to talk about it. Mrs. Lovett, my elderly ninth-grade algebra
teacher—with her dyed blue hair, thick glasses and nasal voice—
would briskly walk toward my desk and stop in front of me to say
in her grandmotherly manner, "Alice Lee Day, would you listen to
me? Stop talking!" Without missing a beat, she would then
return to the blackboard and continue to teach.

Listening to God has been a rather difficult discipline in my
prayer life; it was always much easier to talk. Thankfully, I have
learned how to listen; and I know that unless I am constantly
communing with Him in a listening attitude, I may miss His soft
and gentle voice. Jesus told us that we would hear His voice if we
would only listen:

> The watchman opens the gate for him, and the sheep
> listen to his voice. He calls his own sheep by name and
> leads them out. When he has brought out all his own, he
> goes on ahead of them, and his sheep follow him because
> they know his voice. But they will never follow a stranger;
> in fact, they will run away from him because they do not
> recognize a stranger's voice (John 10:3-5, *NIV*).

In *Beyond the Veil*, I wrote, "Some Christians live as though God wrote a best-seller, the Bible, and then retired! They act as if He has left what happens here totally up to us. But the truth is that God is very active upon the earth! He is fulfilling biblical prophecy daily, finishing the work that He began. His purposes are coming to pass! He is a living, loving, relational God who speaks today! He never stopped speaking! We simply stopped listening. Do you have a yearning for God that burns so deeply within you that your soul is crying out to hear His voice?"[1]

The voice of the Holy Spirit is so soft that unless we are sensitive to Him we will miss His guidance. Even worse, unless we are listening carefully, we may grieve Him and never know it. Consider the reasons why we should listen for the Holy Spirit's voice:

- He is the one who *confirms* to us that we are born-again (see Rom. 8:16).
- He is our *guide* who tells us where we are to go and what we are to say and do (see Rom. 8:14).
- He is our *revelator* who reveals Christ and the Father to us (see John 14:26; 15:26).
- The Spirit of God is our *helper in intercession*. When we don't know how to pray, He prays for us (see Rom. 8:26).
- The Holy Spirit *convicts* us of sin (see John 16:8). He *teaches* us the truth about our future (see John 16:13).

One reason some of us struggle to hear God is because we are not expectant. We ask, but we don't ask in faith expecting to hear Him! Another reason we don't hear is because we haven't predetermined that we will obey Him. The Scripture says, "and his sheep follow him because they know his voice" (John 10:4, *NIV*). It is more than hearing; it is hearing so that we might follow!

When the Lord speaks to you, there is a process that follows; when light is received, more light is given. If you hear and obey the instructions the Lord gives to you, He is pleased to show you more. But if you do not act upon the revelation you have received, then the Lord will withhold revelation until you are once again obedient. Unfortunately, should you quench the Holy Spirit through disobedience, you will go no further in hearing His voice. You can return to a place of intimacy by repenting and turning away from your disobedience to follow Him once more.

If your testimony has been reduced to only speaking of the past—"when I *saw* this" or "when God *did* that"—then you're living off what Jesus said and did yesterday instead of what He is saying and doing today. You must commune with Him regularly to keep your testimony from becoming past tense. He will not lead you into deeper things until you return to seeking His voice.

When it comes to prayer, have you been more of a talker than a listener? Ask the Father right now when you might have received His instructions but didn't listen and obey. Then repent and take action. The result will be new revelation from Him!

Note
1. Alice Smith, *Beyond the Veil* (Ventura, CA: Regal Books, 1997), p. 78.

His Still, Small Voice

*I have been crucified with Christ; it is no longer I who live,
but Christ lives in me; and the life which I now live in
the flesh I live by faith in the Son of God, who
loved me and gave Himself for me.*

GALATIANS 2:20

Many Christians have never developed the ability to distinguish between the loud, boisterous voice of self and the quiet, still voice of the Spirit of God. Yet the language of the two is incompatible. Self-love whispers in your ear; God speaks directly to the heart. Self is restless, eager to do its own thing recklessly. The Holy Spirit speaks a few words in a gentle and mild voice. As soon as you regularly tune in to the loud voice of self, you will no longer be able to hear the soft tones of the Holy Spirit.

Isn't it interesting that pride permeates our churches because of the self's soulish need for flattery? To feel that it has succeeded, the soul must be flattered, paid attention to, recognized and honored. The result is that thousands of people move each year from church to church, ministry to ministry, looking for someone who will honor them.

Those who become absorbed in self generate unhealthy soulish and mental exercises that are destructive to their Christian walk and relationships. Some telltale signs are found in thoughts such as *Am I important to God?* or *Does the pastor even notice me?* Such questions insult the grace and love of God and shout about pride and self-absorption.

God wants to fill us with Himself completely. For that to happen we must first be emptied of self—we must let the proud nonsense of self-love be quieted so that in the stillness of our hearts we may listen to our heavenly Father's words of love.

It is ironic that self-centeredness—the source of our faults—is also what hides our faults. While on this earth, we can understand only in part (see 1 Cor. 13:12). All the more reason to cultivate hearing God's voice. If we do this, we can hear Him whisper that we should reckon ourselves dead to sin (see Rom. 6:11). Unless we see ourselves from the light of God's perspective, we won't really know the truth about ourselves. But if we ask the Holy Spirit to help us, He will show us what we are really like.

This knowledge is for our good, because the Father's love is pure; He loves you with neither prejudice nor flattery. He never shows you your weakness without giving you the courage to face it in order to change. Isn't He amazing? He will not dump all of our imperfections on us at once but will show them to us one by one as we are able to deal with them. There is no condemnation to those who are in Christ Jesus (see Rom. 8:1), so beware lest this devotional cause you to focus on self-pity. Without the heavenly Father's grace, we would surely all fall into despair and discouragement.

Will you allow the Spirit of God to root out any self-focus that dominates your thoughts, actions and attitudes? Through that process He will cleanse you of sin and heal you from the inside out. Once change begins to operate in you, then the mercy of God will be extended to others through you, manifested in consideration and graciousness toward others. For the love of God is kind, considerate and patient. His immeasurable grace leads us out of our self-nature one step at a time.

Although the Holy Spirit is no stranger to your spirit, He will never fight for attention. He speaks within the silent halls of your heart. If the Holy Spirit has had to sit silently for some time due to the noisy clamor of the self's voice, then His voice may sound unfamiliar to you at first. Hearing God's voice is not something mystical. The Father speaks to you from the inside out, from your spirit to your mind. The devil speaks from the outside in, from your five senses—what you hear, see, touch, smell and taste—to your mind. Yield to the tender voice of the Lord deep within you and He will speak. Accept what He desires to show you. If you seek His face, He will show you everything you need to know about yourself. Are you ready to discard the self-love that produces deadness in your prayer life? Then go before the Lord in silence. Listen to His quiet voice. When you hear that still, small voice within your heart, it is the Holy Spirit speaking.

Love Notes

He brought me to the banqueting house, and his banner over me was love.

SONG OF SOLOMON 2:4

One of my favorite things to do when I was a young mother was to rock my babies. Even as they grew older, they wanted me to rock them in our favorite rocking chair. It was our special time of quiet intimacy together.

Our youngest child, Ashlee, has always been openly affectionate. When she was a baby, at night she would snuggle real close to my body and lay across my chest, pulling her legs up under her in a fetal position. Other times she would wrap her little arms around my neck and play with my hair and my earrings as I sang praise and worship songs over her until she fell fast asleep. The memories of those early days of our children's lives are so precious. Each baby is so different—so unique in God's eyes.

Just as a mother cherishes her precious baby, the heavenly Father cherishes you and me. Each one of us is unique to the Father. He knows us intimately and loves each of us dearly. He longs to look into our faces and to hold us in the comforting arms of His great love. Some of us actually fear Him, but that's because we misunderstand who He really is. A number of us have difficulty receiving His love because of the negative father image we have due to past mental, emotional or physical abuse. The Father isn't partial in His love. He loves us equally, for God is love (see 1 John 4:8). The love of God is consistent, faithful, unending—and undeserved. Totally unearned! Amazingly, before we ever knew Him, and when we were living in our sin, aliens to His nature and enemies of His kingdom, He loved us (see Rom. 5:8,10)! Ephesians 3:19 tells us "to know the love of Christ which passes knowledge; that you may be filled with all the fullness of God."

Our daughter Julie married an Israeli man. The first of their three children is Adriel, which in Hebrew means "a strong tower." I remember visiting them one day after Julie and her husband had moved to Houston. At the time, Adriel was about two years old. We were sitting in the living room visiting when Adriel's dad, Barach, left the room to answer the phone. The baby continued to play in the middle of the floor, not really concerned that his dad had left the room. Yet a few minutes later, as Barach came back into the living room, our sweet, precious grandson stood up and began to walk quickly toward his daddy. His deep brown eyes lit up, and a smile spread across his face. With his hands straight up in the air, he rushed to Barach, saying, "Abba, Abba," the Hebrew word for "daddy." As his daddy picked him up, baby Adriel tightly hugged his father in a simple act of love. Eddie and I felt great emotion as we witnessed this profound illustration of the larger picture.

Our heavenly Abba longs for us to run to Him with our hands extended in delight. But often we are too busy or too distracted with other things to be bothered with Him. We need to draw close to the One who loves in a way no one else ever could. The Greek word for God's unfailing, selfless love is *agape*. God agapes us! And His arms are extended toward us as we cry, "Abba, Father!"

I love the teaching of J. I. Packer. He is one of the greatest men of God from our era. In his book *Knowing God,* he eloquently writes:

What matters supremely . . . is not, in the last analysis, the fact that I know God, but the larger fact which underlies it—that He knows me. I am graven on the palms of His hands. I am never out of His mind. All my knowledge of Him depends on His sustained initiative in knowing me. I know Him because He first knew me, and continues to know me. He knows me as a friend, one who loves me; and there is no moment when His eye is off me, or falters. This is the momentous knowledge. There is unspeakable comfort . . . in knowing that God is constantly taking knowledge of me in love and watching over me for my good. There is tremendous relief in knowing that His love is utterly realistic; based at every point on prior knowledge of the worst about me, so that no discovery now can disillusion Him about me, in the way I am so often disillusioned about myself, and quench His determination to bless me.[1]

What love! The love notes of God are written in the memories of our hearts. Can you recall the times when the heavenly Father reached out and lifted you up into His arms after some tremendous disappointment? Or when the betrayal of one you loved hurt so deeply that eating or sleeping eluded you?

The cherished moments of rocking my children are over. Time passes so quickly, doesn't it? Yet, my friend, neither time nor age will ever interfere with the privilege we have to crawl into our heavenly Father's lap, allowing Him to speak His love notes into our hearts. Is it time for you to run to your heavenly Daddy with arms outstretched? Do it now!

Note

1. J. I. Packer, *Knowing God*, quoted in Charles Swindoll, *The Tale of the Tardy Oxcart* (Nashville, TN: Word Publishing, 1998), p. 236.

Handling Crisis

*So the LORD spoke to Moses face to face, as a man
speaks to his friend.*

EXODUS 33:11

Have you ever been in a crisis when you knew the Lord was
ready and waiting to give you victory, but you blew it? You could
have trusted and praised Him for the situation, but instead, you
complained. Has that ever happened to you? It has to me.

When we don't handle a crisis well, often the Father engi-
neers the crisis again to give us another opportunity to pass the
test. But when we wait for this replay to get it right, we often are
not as committed to learn the lesson as the first time, and we will
have less discernment of what God is doing and more humilia-
tion from not having obeyed. If we continue to grieve the Holy
Spirit, there will come a time when we become numb to the
crisis—choosing to simply blame the devil for our own lack of
obedience.

God sometimes has to shake areas in our lives for our own
good and to give us the opportunity to move closer to Him. If we
continue to resist the work of the Lord, the result will be emotional turmoil and spiritual emptiness.

Now the good news! If we face the crisis with humility, all
the while praising God for the opportunity to become more like
Him, then the testimony of our lives will reflect Christ's likeness
to others. Gloriously, we are promoted to new levels of victory
and joy because in our hearts we know that we have stood strong
in faith regardless of the crisis.

Can you imagine the tension Moses must have felt when he asked for God's presence to go with him as he led the children of Israel into the Promised Land? Here is Moses' prayer and God's response:

> "Now therefore, I pray, if I have found grace in Your sight, show me now Your way, that I may know You and that I may find grace in Your sight. And consider that this nation is Your people." And He said, "My Presence will go with you, and I will give you rest." Then he said to Him, "If Your Presence does not go with us, do not bring us up from here" (Exod. 33:13-15).

Moses' crisis was that he had to lead millions of people from slavery, through a wilderness, before bringing them to a place of promise. He handled the crisis well, because he would not go forward without the presence of the Lord. You, too, may be afraid to move forward when facing a crisis. Questions invade your mind: *Did God really tell me to do this? What happens if I fail?*

Many times during a crisis I have felt painfully disturbed, distracted and unsure. It's as if the waves and billows of God's providential timing are sweeping over me, yet I am not prepared for them. Moses didn't feel prepared to face his crisis either. Yet God told him, "So it shall be, while My glory passes by, that I will put you in the cleft of the rock, and will cover you with My hand while I pass by. Then I will take away My hand, and you shall see My back; but My face shall not be seen" (Exod. 33:22-23).

Perhaps you have an unconscious fear that if you pursue the Lord and begin to receive His friendship in a deeper way, it may cost you more than you are willing to pay. We long for more of His presence, yet we know that to whom much is given, much is required. Are you thinking that maybe the responsibility could be so great that if you disobeyed or did something stupid during the crunch time, you would be disqualified for future ministry opportunities? Relax. The Lord is a good God, and He desires for us to stay humble, teachable and always hungry for more of Him. As long as you continue to seek His face, you have nothing to worry about.

To learn God's ways can be costly; yet to live without knowing His ways will always cost you more! Exodus 33:11 records that God spoke to Moses face-to-face, as one would speak to a friend. Imagine the joy of hearing the Father call you His friend, too! Don't you want to hear that? I sure do.

Persevering Prayer

Won't God grant his chosen people justice when they cry out to him day and night? Is he slow to help them?

LUKE 18:7, ISV

Have you experienced times—or even extended seasons—when your prayer life seemed more like the Sahara desert than the life-giving oasis it should be? When that happens, the problem isn't on the Father's end of the line—it's on yours.

Many people of prayer act as though they can't proceed in daily living until they get a "word from God." They have heard others talk about the Lord's speaking to them to the point that they think they should hear from God continually. But God is not a chatterbox. Novice Christians who claim they are hearing from God on a daily basis are usually known for talking much, not for their effectiveness in the Kingdom. Resist the temptation to push the Lord in prayer, demanding that He come to you on your terms.

If you will walk according to the truth of God's Word, He will surprise you with profound, life-changing words that will extend His kingdom through your life. But He won't do so if you keep pressing Him to speak. You may get "words," but they won't necessarily be from the Lord. (The enemy is often anxious to speak words to those who lack spiritual discernment.) God wants you to be faithful in the mundane things of life—He wants you to persevere—so that when the extraordinary happens, you will have enough character to bear it without pride.

Ever notice how a practiced long-distance runner knows when to pace himself and when it's time to dig in and push? Runners call this perceived exertion. "To perceive" something is to be aware of it by the senses. "To exert" is to push ahead in an extraordinary way. So at that inevitable point in the critical race, when the runner feels exhausted, in pain, and feels tempted to quit, he or she has been trained to exert an explosive effort to push beyond those thoughts or feelings. The endorphins kick in, stimulating the body, and the runner wins the race!

This is exactly what you need to do in the seemingly dry seasons of prayer. When you pray, sometimes you suddenly "hit the wall," and distractions, fatigue and drowsiness come over you. You feel weighed down, unfocused and out of it. That's when the trained and disciplined intercessor applies perceived exertion. He or she begins to exert extra effort—pacing the floor, praying aloud, playing praise and worship music, praying in your prayer language, reading Scripture aloud or pressing in with added emotion.

There are also times when the Lord removes His manifested presence so that you will exert yourself to run after Him. Struggle can be very good if you don't give up. But don't push for an expected response from Jesus. You are running in prayer for the sheer faithfulness of it. The benefits may come later.

Runners win races by pushing the boundaries and stressing their muscles; the exertion builds up and tones their bodies. In a similar way, an intercessor's spiritual muscles are strengthened when he or she runs hard after the Lord. This ebb and flow of seeking and finding the Lord allows us to stay tender, compassionate and sympathetic to others who find prayer difficult. But be forewarned: When you try too hard, without setting a pace and faithfully running it, your flesh will take over and perform whether the

Lord is present or not. You can easily perform ministry—you can pray or conduct any church activity—apart from the Holy Spirit. So be careful that you guard your heart from this happening.

Not every prayer time is a blazing success. There are times when the Lord simply won't let you catch Him because He will never allow you to take Him for granted. After all, if Jesus allowed you to win every time, He would be predictable, and in your boredom you would discontinue the pursuit.

I am talking about more than emotions here. Certainly you should begin in prayer by using your emotions, but then you shift into a spirit-to-Spirit engagement with the Almighty! Just as trained runners run with ease—their movements almost effortless—so life-giving intercessory prayer comes from the depth of your spirit. You enter His Holy of Holies and invite Him into yours!

Your relationship with God is to be a delightful adventure! A colorful phrase from Song of Solomon reveals the kind of delight that should be a hallmark of our pursuit of the Lord: "Make haste, my beloved, and be like a gazelle or a young stag on the mountains of spices" (8:14). Don't be anxious or afraid; run to Jesus with love words today. Your heavenly lover delights in the chase!

The DEVELOPMENT

DEVELOPMENT: TO BRING TO FULFILLMENT; TO EXPAND OR
ENLARGE; TO AID IN THE GROWTH OF; TO STRENGTHEN.
TO IMPROVE THE QUALITY OF; TO REFINE.

*Where do we go from here? We were created for
intimacy with God. When we continue to make our
daily pilgrimage beyond the veil in acknowledgment of
His lordship, we will be conformed into the likeness
of Jesus as we experience transformation by way of
adoration! Enjoy the lover of your soul—Jesus Christ!*

God's Prayer Partner

*The eyes of the LORD are on the righteous and his
ears are attentive to their cry.*

PSALM 34:15, *NIV*

Mass confusion reigned as the sound of many voices echoed
across the valley. The tribes of Israel loudly and sullenly complained that they were sick of the manna, that they longed for
meat and veggies, and that they had eaten *much* better food as
slaves. Suddenly, from his place of prayer, Moses, God's rugged
warrior, wearily aired his frustration: "God, why are You picking
on me? Why do You give me the burden of a people like this? Are
they my children? Am I their father? Am I to nurse these sissy
babies until we get to the land You've promised us? This nation
is too heavy for me to bear!" (see Num. 11).

Moments later the Lord instructed Moses to gather 70 of
Israel's elders to help him bear the burden of leadership.
According to verse 25 (*NIV*), "When the Spirit rested on them,
they prophesied." Several of the men, who had not been present
in the meeting, also prophesied. Young Joshua was concerned.
He said, "'Moses, my lord, stop them!' But Moses replied, 'Are
you jealous for my sake? I wish that all the LORD's people were
prophets and that the LORD would put his Spirit on them!'" (vv.
28-29, *NIV*).

You see, prophecy and intercession go together. The prophetic intercessor speaks the message of the Lord in intercessory

prayer. In essence, he or she reminds God of His own Word.

> The word of the LORD came to me: "Son of man, speak
> to your countrymen and say to them: 'When I bring the
> sword against a land, and the people of the land choose
> one of their men and make him their watchman, and he
> sees the sword coming against the land and blows the
> trumpet to warn the people, then if anyone hears the
> trumpet but does not take warning and the sword comes
> and takes his life, his blood will be on his own head.
> Since he heard the sound of the trumpet, but did not
> take warning, his blood will be on his own head. If he
> had taken warning, he would have saved himself. But if
> the watchman sees the sword coming and does not blow
> the trumpet to warn the people and the sword comes
> and takes the life of one of them, that man will be taken
> away because of his sin, but I will hold the watchman
> accountable for his blood.' Son of man, I have made you
> a watchman for the house of Israel; so hear the word I
> speak and give them warning from me" (Ezek. 33:1-7,
> *NIV*).

Was Ezekiel a prophet or an intercessor? He was both. Ezekiel both heard and spoke God's warnings. When the Lord warns us of some impending disaster, we should not assume that He desires it to happen. Sometimes the Lord reveals the enemy's plan to us so that we can war against it. Prophetic intercession is the ability to pray in faith about something revealed to us by the Holy Spirit, without any natural knowledge.

The primary Old Testament Hebrew word for the word "prophet" is *nabi'*, which comes from the verb *naba'*. Naba' can be translated as "to bubble up" or "boil forth."[1] One of the words translated as "prophecy" is *massa'*; it also means "burden."[2]

Massa' signifies the breaking forth of the burden of God from the innermost parts. An intercessor's task is to state the cause for another in prayer, and a prophet's task is to announce a message from God. In prophetic intercession the two blend together. When in prayer, a prophetic intercessor states the cause of another and prays God's revelation concerning it into reality.

Prophetic intercessors prophesy as they pray. If you are an intuitive and sensitive person, you probably often pray prophetically and don't even realize it. You are so in tune with the Lord that you are praying the heart of God!

Psalm 34:15-17 (*NIV*) reads, "The eyes of the LORD are on the righteous and his ears are attentive to their cry; the face of the LORD is against those who do evil, to cut off the memory of them from the earth. The righteous cry out, and the LORD hears them; he delivers them from all their troubles."

If God sees and hears the prayers of the righteous, then we can trust Him to intervene on our behalf, can't we? After all, God desires to deal mercifully with us. "Let the wicked forsake his way and the evil man his thoughts. Let him turn to the LORD, and he will have mercy on him, and to our God, for he will freely pardon" (Isa. 55:7, *NIV*).

In Numbers 12:1-8, we see some of the ways that God speaks to men. God speaks to us in dreams, subconscious revelation, trances, closed visions, open visions and in an audible voice, as He spoke to Aaron, Miriam and Moses.

Once you receive prophetic insight, ask the Holy Spirit for illumination. You want to pray in faith, not presumption. Presumption is based on assumptions; faith is based on known truth. Faith is never a leap in the dark; it is always a step in the light!

Remain teachable in this area of hearing God's voice. No one likes a know-it-all. Scripture instructs us: "Be self-controlled and alert. Your enemy the devil prowls around like a roaring lion looking for someone to devour" (1 Pet. 5:8, *NIV*). Walk in godly accountability, or you may be the one devoured!

Count on this: If you hear and obey God in prophetic intercession, you will be criticized for being illogical. It requires perseverance to fulfill prophetic assignments. Be prepared for some to accuse you of missing God or misinterpreting what He has said. You're in good company when you consider the biblical stories of the Israelites who boldly marched around Jericho seven times; the young boy who confidently took five small stones to fight a giant; the leper who dutifully bathed his body in a muddy river to get healed; the young men who obediently stepped into a fiery furnace and came out again without even the smell of scorched clothing. These actions were anything *but* reasonable, yet see what happened when these people heard God's voice and obeyed!

Ask the Lord to teach you how to pray prophetically. Begin with the little assignments He gives you, and soon your vision will increase.

Notes

1. R. Laird Harris, Gleason L. Archer, Jr., and Bruce K. Waltke, eds. *Theological Wordbook of the Old Testament,* vol. 2 (Chicago: Moody Press, 1980), p. 544.
2. Francis Brown, S. R. Driver and Charles A. Briggs. *The Brown-Driver-Briggs Hebrew and English Lexicon* (1906; reprint, Peabody, MA: Hendrickson Publishers, 1996), p. 672.

Clashing Kingdoms

*For we do not wrestle against flesh and blood, but against
principalities, against powers, against the rulers of the
darkness of this age, against spiritual hosts of
wickedness in the heavenly places.*

EPHESIANS 6:12

When we were local church pastors, my husband, Eddie,
once said during a teaching session, "One of the key characteristics of an intercessor with a spiritual warfare calling is a sense of
'holy dissatisfaction.'" At that comment, Darla, one of our stronger intercessors, gasped aloud, "That's it!" Eddie asked her what
might be wrong. She explained with tears of relief, "All my life my
family has said of me, 'You are never satisfied.' And they are right."

David F. Wells, a professor of historical and systematic theology, states:

> What then, is the nature of petitionary prayer? It is, in
> essence, rebellion—rebellion against the world in its fallenness, the absolute and undying refusal to accept as
> normal what is pervasively abnormal. It is, in this its
> negative aspect, the refusal of every agenda, every
> scheme, every interpretation that is at odds with the
> norm as originally established by God.[1]

I envision that a day will come when thousands of intercessors with militant, reckless abandonment for Jesus will *stand up* for the lost, *stand against* the powers of darkness and *stand for* the kingdom of God. They will be radical. John the Baptist was radical! Paul was radical! Elijah was radical! Are you radical when it comes to prayer?[2]

In this ancient battle of God's kingdom against Satan's kingdom, there is a world at stake. It is a battle for worshipers, which means that the souls of men and women, boys and girls are on the line. Satan's ground-level victories can be seen in the lives of those who have sold themselves out to habitual sin—and worse—those who because of sin, trauma and generational iniquity are already demonized (influenced or controlled by demonic spirits). Satan's global victories are evident in the billions of people around the world who are still trapped in darkness due to territorial spiritual bondage.

But the earth is the Lord's. Not only did He create it, but from the thief who stole it He also bought it back by the blood of His own sinless Son, Jesus. The earth and all who live in it are the Lord's (see Ps. 24:1).

In this war we have one strategic advantage that we often overlook. Our providential God has allowed us to read the last chapter of history. We already know how it will turn out. God says the earth shall be filled with the knowledge of His glory as the waters cover the seas (see Hab. 2:14)! That means the streets of your hometown; the homes in your neighborhood; the schools, churches and business establishments in your city are going to be filled with the knowledge of His glory! We don't pray with any question about how this is all going to turn out! We pray in faith, believing that what God has said, He will do.

The Lord cannot empower us—He cannot anoint us or truly authorize us to stand against the works of darkness on Earth—until we have first dealt with the darkness in our own lives. It is in our minds, our hearts, our lives and our relationships that the first victories must be won. We can't pull down a stronghold with one hand and hold it up with the other. That is why our righteous lives must be examples to the kingdom of darkness. After all, King David the warrior didn't begin by taking cities. Oh, no. He began defeating lions and bears and then graduated to conquering giants (Goliath). Out of David's faithfulness to God, he was given the authority to conquer cities and nations!

The day will soon come when a purified and unified Church stands together as one Bride of Christ and announces to Satan, "No more!" At that point, Christ has promised us that hell's gates will not be able to stand. We are strategic people living at a strategic moment in history. Will you enlist for battle?

History records that Frederick the Great wrote to one of his generals, "I send you with 60,000 men against the enemy." Upon numbering the troops, however, it was found that there were only 50,000. The general expressed surprise at such a mistake on the part of his sovereign. Frederick's reply was, "I counted on you for 10,000 men!" How much time can the Lord Jesus count on from you to pray for the many souls who need to hear the gospel?[3]

If you find it difficult to be satisfied with what you see and sense around you, it's likely that God is calling you to battle in prayer for what ought to be. Don't wait to be drafted—enlist now!

Notes

1. David F. Wells, *Perspectives on the World Christian Movement* (Pasadena, CA: William Carey Library, 1981), p. 124.
2. Alice Smith, *Beyond the Veil* (Ventura, CA: Regal Books, 1997), p. 41.
3. Ibid., p. 37.

Exercising Authority

Finally, my brethren, be strong in the Lord and in the power of His might. Put on the whole armor of God, that you may be able to stand against the wiles of the devil.

EPHESIANS 6:10-11

$\mathcal{I}$ have always been a warrior. When I was a teenager, my friends nicknamed me Bulldog. Just as a bulldog will grab and hold the pant leg of its victim, I will take a prayer issue and hang on to it until I see something happen. However, untrained and undisciplined warriors can be a danger to themselves and to others—as I was during my earlier years.

In the 1980s, I began to research the history of the city in which we live. The nature of the spiritual darkness we were facing soon became clear to me. My heart burned in prayer for Houston—America's fourth largest city. With the tenacity of a bulldog I sought the Lord, intent on finding out what territorial spirits held our city in their grip. Daily I begged the Lord for insight.

One winter morning during prayer, I felt the Lord speak to me about my city's spiritual condition. I sensed that He was telling me the names of the demonic princes that are the "puppet masters" assigned to carry out Satan's bidding. They rule in the affairs of men through wicked and deceived leaders.

Arrogantly (although I didn't realize it at the time), I began to bark at the principalities that hindered our city. From my prayer closet I zealously attacked them in fervent warfare. "In the name of Jesus, you spirit of _____, I command you to get out of Houston. We don't want you here. I stand against your every scheme to steal, kill and destroy."

After several weeks of ranting and raving against these workers of darkness, their counterattack came against me like a nuclear blast. I came within 10 hours of dying from peritonitis of the spleen and liver. That's not all. Eddie and I had six major surgeries in 14 months, and three of them weren't covered by insurance. Our savings had been depleted, and we were on the brink of losing our home. With a growing family, a new baby and a young church that had just lost its first pastor, I was in a terrible place. To the demons' delight, the church was struggling, our family was struggling, and I was struggling.

"And it came to pass," written 446 times in the Bible, is one of my favorite phrases in Scripture! Thankfully, painful times do pass, and eventually the dust settled around us. I believed that all of this persecution from the powers of darkness had come because I was such a godly person. Boy, was I wrong!

One morning, I was praying about all that we had experienced. The Lord spoke so clearly to my heart that I can almost hear the echo of His voice to this day. He said to me, "Alice, I told you the names of the spirits over Houston, but you never asked Me what you were to do with the revelation." I could hardly believe it! Now I know that diagnosis doesn't necessarily equal assignment! Knowing what is wrong and being told to correct it are two completely different issues.

Has Christ given us authority to deal with the enemy? Absolutely He has! But the authority given to us is ambassadorial, not carte blanche. We are not called to be spiritual Rambos, or armies of one. We are called to be disciplined warriors who explicitly follow the orders of our Commander-in-Chief and the Lord of Hosts—the Lord Jesus Christ. Our Lord's timing and His assignment of us to the battle are critical. To engage the enemy without His direction is presumptuous at best. I had the best of intentions, but with arrogance and pride I found myself fighting for my life in a battle I had picked on my own. I repented to the Lord and then to Eddie. It was a costly lesson, but one I will never forget.

My preacher husband often says, "We have two teachers in life: mentors and mistakes. We choose whether we will learn from our mistakes or from our mentors." I trust I am your mentor today. Please take this issue to heart and learn from this bull-dog!

Victory over Adversity

Yet in all these things we are more than conquerors
through Him who loved us.

ROMANS 8:37

⟊nce there was a farmer whose old mule accidentally fell into the farmer's dry well. The farmer heard the mule braying (or whatever mules do when they fall into dry wells). After carefully assessing the situation, the farmer sympathized with the mule but decided that neither the mule nor the dry well was worth saving.

Instead, he called his neighbors together, told them what had happened and enlisted their help in hauling dirt to bury the old mule in the well and put him out of his misery.

At first the mule was hysterical. But as the farmer and his neighbors continued to shovel the dirt into the well, a thought struck the mule. It suddenly dawned on him that every time a shovel of dirt landed on his back he should shake it off and step up! This he did, blow after blow.

"Shake it off and step up . . . shake it off and step up . . . shake it off and step up," he repeated to encourage himself. No matter how painful the blows or distressing the situation, the old mule fought off his panic and just kept right on shaking off the dirt and stepping up.

You're probably ahead of the story by now. It wasn't long

before the old mule, battered and exhausted, stepped triumphantly over the wall of the well. What was intended to bury him had actually buoyed him—all because of the manner in which he handled his adversity!

All of us are going to face life's hardships. When we do, we can either cave in or we can climb out. We can either submit to anxiety—which is to call into question the integrity of our God—or we can face our problems positively and refuse to give in to panic, worry or self-pity. Rather than bury us, life's adversities can actually serve to benefit us!

Within the burden you now carry lie the seeds of your Kingdom destiny. The greater the burden you carry, the greater the potential of your Kingdom purpose to be fulfilled. I know it's hard to face the painful situation you are in without seeing yourself bruised and buried. If you are willing to step over the pain and step up to new levels of victory, then you are on your way to the fulfillment of your destiny in Christ. It is in carrying your burdens that you will find your destiny. If you never press into the throne of God in prayer to address your greatest pain, then you will live an unfulfilled life. Sadly, many Christians are running from their burdens. God, however, is asking us not to run from them but to shake them off and step up each time the blows of life come. He's asking us to wrestle victory out of defeat and to allow the problems of life to become our stepping-stones rather than stumbling blocks.

The apostle Paul was certainly troubled with bad days. He once said, "When we came to Macedonia, our bodies had no rest, but we were troubled on every side. Outside were conflicts, inside were fears" (2 Cor. 7:5). Wow! Paul was familiar with life's problems. This godly man was troubled and fearful. In fact, at one point it seemed that all of Asia had turned against Paul. He wrote, "The more abundantly I love you, the less I am loved" (2 Cor. 12:15).

To be sure, our troubles and burdens are nothing compared to what Paul endured. But Paul never gave in to his feelings of despair and temptations. He expressed his pain but pressed on beyond it. In his most difficult time, he testified, "I am filled with comfort. I am exceedingly joyful in all our tribulation" (2 Cor. 7:4). And he continued by saying, "God, who comforts the downcast, comforted us" (v. 6). Perhaps one reason Paul spoke these words was to exhort himself to do the right thing.

Although your burdens may seem at times as if they will bury you, they could forge the path for your greatest victory. Your adversity is your opportunity to shake it off and step up. As you do, you will eventually step out of the grave of despair, just as the old mule did. And better still, you will step into the realization of your Kingdom destiny. Remember Paul's exhortation to give "thanks always for all things to God the Father in the name of our Lord Jesus Christ" (Eph. 5:20). What are you waiting for? Begin to thank the Lord right now.

G~R~A~C~E

*Do you despise the riches of His goodness, forbearance, and
longsuffering, not knowing that the goodness of
God leads you to repentance?*

ROMANS 2:4

One evening, as Eddie and I watched television talk-show host
Larry King interview an old friend of ours whom we hadn't seen
in more than 20 years, we became increasingly saddened by our
friend's words and demeanor. He came across as extremely intol-
erant and judgmental. At one point, Eddie turned to me and
said in a subdued voice, "Honey, can you imagine anyone wanting to spend a weekend in a mountain cabin with him?"

Isn't it ironic how we can apply our own religious rules and
regulations once we have received Christ?! Yet our position in
Christ is only because of God's grace and mercy. Think about it:
Not one of us received this great salvation by complying with a
set of rules or standards. Each of us was drawn into Christ's
kingdom by His incomparable and unconditional love. There is
a well-known acronym G-R-A-C-E, which stands for God's
Riches at Christ's Expense. When we receive grace from God,
there isn't one thing we can do to deserve it!

Aren't you glad that God doesn't make clones? He orches-
trates your life without demanding that everyone else follow
your same path. Likewise, we need to be tolerant of other
Christians who don't look, act, dress and talk like us. We need to
allow God to be as original with their circumstances as He has
been with ours. After all, what is required to bring one Christian
into full surrender, another person would reject. God knows the

heart, and He is the one who conforms a person into His image.

The error of holding others to a false standard of behavior and judging them when they fail to meet that standard is not limited to the fellowship of believers. What about those who don't yet know Christ? My heart grieves when I see members of the Church isolate themselves from society by picketing abortion clinics with mean-spirited signs and protesting rock concerts with "You're going to hell" posters, and then wonder why the world doesn't respond to Jesus. It appears to me that we are skilled at alienating the very people we should be reaching—people for whom Christ died!

The heartbreaking truth is that too often the lost world assumes that Christ has nothing to offer them because Christianity appears to be just another set of rules to keep. Yet the Lord Himself has told us that rule keeping doesn't please Him. In fact, it sickens Him! He says that "even our best actions are filthy through and through" (Isa. 64:6, *TEV*).

Loving the lost is our job; transforming the lost is God's job. If we will take off our judge's robe, lay down our gavel and climb down from the bench, we can then come alongside those who do not know Jesus and be their defense attorney in prayer. Satan wants to prosecute, judge and declare a sentence of death on them. We can plead in prayer for their lives! After all, James 2:13 says, "Mercy triumphs over judgment!"

When we walk in humility and grace, we can offer grace and mercy to both our fellow believers and to those who don't yet know Christ. When we love people as God loves them, the joy of the Lord springs from our lives as a well of living water that bubbles up to refresh and revive thirsty souls.

Go to God in prayer, asking the Holy Spirit to help you understand in a deep way what G-R-A-C-E means. If there are any areas of your life in which you have been living by the letter rather than the spirit of the law, ask God to show you how to reflect His grace and mercy toward your family and friends, toward fellow believers and toward those who don't know Jesus.

A story was told to me about a lady who complained to a friend visiting her that her next-door neighbor was a poor housekeeper, her children were dirty, her house was filthy and one was almost disgraced by living near her. "Just look," she said, "at those filthy clothes she has hung out on the line. See the black streaks up and down those sheets and pillowcases?" The friend stepped to the window, raised the sash and looked out. "It appears, my dear, that the clothes are perfectly clean. The streaks that you see are on your own window."

Let's stop setting standards for each other. Although awareness of judgmentalism may not come to you immediately, because awareness requires a revelation to the heart, if you have a humble and submissive heart, in time the Lord will reveal a truth that without a doubt is life-changing. Not only will you be changed, but those who know you will also be affected.

Kingdom Advancement

For we walk by faith, not by sight.

2 CORINTHIANS 5:7

Who would you call in a spiritual emergency? Do you have an Elijah—someone whom God has placed in your life as a mentor and role model? Although God provides us Elijahs, in due time we learn that we must not continue to lean on them. God gives us mentors for a reason, but He also gives them for a season. His ultimate desire for us is that we stand on our own. The day will come—if it hasn't already—for you to leave the safety and security of the nest and fly.

Consider the partnership of Elijah and Elisha. Three times Elijah made plans to leave; and three times Elisha replied, "As the LORD lives, and as your soul lives, I will not leave you!" (2 Kings 2:2,4,6). He admired and emulated Elijah. He didn't want his friend and mentor to leave. But there would come a time when Elijah would have to go.

At some point, like Elisha experienced, your Elijah will have to leave. It is painful but predictable, and it's God's plan. You must not refuse to release your Elijah or else you will forfeit your full Kingdom potential.

When Elijah ascended in a chariot of fire, Elisha found himself alone. He returned to the Jordan River, which is symbolic of death and separation. "Crossing Jordan" means death to the old and birth to the new opportunities and responsibilities. Your Jordan experiences are those in which you must take the responsibility to walk out what your Elijahs have taught you. When you are alone, the Jordan, once a very familiar place, will seem overwhelming and impossible to cross.

Some would wrongly conclude that troubles dissipate when one becomes a Christian. Not so. God does not remove trouble; rather, He empowers us to overcome in the midst of it. After all, without trials there would never be triumph. There is no victory without war, and there is no war without an enemy. Strangely, trouble is our friend. Trouble brings us to total dependency upon Christ. Prepare to cross your own Jordans, confront your own giants and gain your own victories.

The usual response to trouble is to say, "I can't." We fail to realize that our tests are tailor-made and the Father always provides a way to bear them (1 Cor. 10:13).

Wasn't God the God of Elisha as well as of Elijah? Even though it seemed overwhelming, Elisha was ready to cross the Jordan alone. And we must make the same journey.

It is important when faced with trouble to keep our focus on Christ. When we focus on our trouble, all of our strength goes to the problem rather than to the solution. At this point, we are not only afflicted by trouble but we are also distracted from our communion with Christ who is the source of our strength. Intimacy with Christ is where you will find the strength to stand. You are to stand in faith, walk by faith and live by faith in the Son of God (see Eph. 6:13-14; Gal. 2:20).

In 2 Kings 2:15, we read that a company of prophets from Jericho were watching Elisha. Inside your heart you long to trust God for the extraordinary, but people are watching. You wish someone else could do the work for you. The thought may come to you as it probably did to Elisha, *Where is my Elijah when I really need him?* Amazingly, if you will press in and be true to the call of God, regardless of your feelings of insecurity and inadequacy or your lack of faith, the Lord will prove Himself to you.

In 2 Kings 2:23-25 we find Elisha being jeered by a large group of young people at Bethel (a portion of the group—42, in fact—were mauled by bears). "Bethel" means "the house of God." Yes, even Christian friends and family may mock your faith or your passion or the level of your commitment. When I was a newly saved teenager, older Christians said, "Alice, after you've been saved awhile, you'll settle down." Today, after more than 37 years, I am more passionately in love with Christ than ever!

Shortly after I began writing my first book, *Beyond the Veil*, a Christian leader told me that I was foolish to think that I could write a book. That statement so intimidated me that I shelved the book for 10 months. However, I couldn't shake the fact that the Lord had spoken to me to write this book. In Christ I found the courage to begin again, and *Beyond the Veil* has become a bestseller. Yes, even in the Church you will find your critics. It's possible that those who have walked with you for years may leave you if the commitment level becomes too difficult for them.

Are you at the end of your endurance? Have you been feeling the need to quit? Don't do it! Your extremity of need is God's opportunity. Stand on His promises. In His time He will disclose the truth and validate you. The fight is not yours; the battle is the Lord's! Practice what the Elijahs in your life have taught you. Put on the mantle of prayer and stand confidently in Christ. Stop looking back for your Elijah to do it for you. Jesus Christ is more than enough!

Don't Give Up!

*And let us not grow weary while doing good, for in due
season we shall reap if we do not lose heart.*

GALATIANS 6:9

Remember the *Peanuts* character Lucy, the bossy little girl
who holds the football for Charlie Brown every football season
so that he can kick the ball? She moves the ball just as Charlie's
foot is about to make contact and sends him sprawling.
Aggravated, yet still trusting, he gets up and tries again. In one
instance Charlie reacts this way: After several attempts, he says
in frustration, "Where do you go to give up?"

Each of us has come to the giving-up place at some point in
our Christian walk. Usually it happens because we don't understand the way God works in our lives, and we find ourselves
tempted to give up on living a dedicated life.

I can think of at least three reasons why we come to this
place of giving up. We can lose heart because of sudden defeating circumstances, because of ongoing disappointments or
because we lose sight of our goal.

The first reason—sudden defeating circumstances—provides
an instant temptation to give up. Consider the story of one
Olympic runner in the 1980s who was on the final leg of a race
when he twisted his ankle and fell. A collective gasp could be
heard throughout the stadium. The athlete got up, ran a short
distance and fell again. Without considering the rules, the runner's father jumped the fence and ran to his son's aid, shouting
for him to stop. The frustrated runner looked at his father and

said, "Dad, I will not give up." But he could run no further. The caring father joined his son and assisted him to the finish line.

Olympic records state that the runner did not finish the race. Not so! Even though the rules stated that for a runner to remain qualified, no other person could touch the runner, the injured Olympian hobbled with his father's help all the way to the finish line—and crossed it!

We can also give in to discouragement because of ongoing disappointments, such as when someone who doesn't deserve it gets ahead of us or when our fondest hopes and dreams get waylaid. You've had it happen, and so have I. You were next in line for the job promotion, but the person who wheeled and dealed got promoted instead. Or perhaps you have a dream or a long-term goal, but others have challenged that dream because of your gender, race or social status! Paul counseled the Galatians about overcoming this kind of discouragement: "You were running a good race. Who cut in on you and kept you from obeying the truth?" (Gal. 5:7-8, *NIV*).

During the 1980 Boston Marathon, Rosie Ruiz was the first woman to cross the finish line. She looked too good for someone who had just run 26 miles. She wasn't sweating or breathing heavily. When questioned, she simply stated how good she had felt that morning. The checkpoint officials did not remember seeing her on the course. Several college students claimed they saw her jump into the race two miles from the finish line. Ruiz was eventually disqualified despite her denials, and second-place finisher Jackie Gareau was elevated to champion.

Can you identify with Jackie? You're running the race and headed for first place, but someone cuts in on you. Although Jackie was eventually given her rightful place, everything doesn't always turn out right. That's when you have to decide if you will stay in the race or give up because someone has deceived you or misled you.

A third giving-up place occurs when we have lost sight of the finish line. It's rare to see a competing athlete turn his or her head to check what's happening behind, because it wastes time and slows them down. Paul says in Philippians 3:12-14: "I press on to take hold of that for which Christ Jesus took hold of me. . . . One thing I do: Forgetting what is behind and straining toward what is ahead, I press on toward the goal to win the prize for which God has called me heavenward in Christ Jesus."

When circumstances press in and take our eyes away from the goal, we need to be reminded that the finish line is still ahead of us. One missionary couple went to the jungles of Africa as young people and ran a marathon by giving 50 years of service to the African people to whom they committed their lives. Now they were returning home—a finish line of sorts. As their ship entered the New York harbor, the elderly couple stood at the deck railing and watched in astonishment while a crowd of dockside people cheered and a band played rousing music. Their hearts were stirred and tears of joy streamed down their cheeks at such an unexpected welcome.

When the boat docked and the passengers began to disembark, the noise of the cheers, whistles and handclapping rose to a high pitch and then lessened as the crowd turned to follow the progress of one man—a famous diplomat who was one of the first passangers to leave the ship. By the time the couple reached the dock, they stood all alone. There was no one to greet them; no one to take them home. Emotion flooded the woman and she began to cry. Her husband pulled her into his arms, stroked her silver hair and tenderly said, "Honey, please don't be sad. Don't you know we're not home yet?" This couple experienced temporary disappointment, but they never lost sight of their eternal goal.

No, it's not easy to remain faithful behind the scenes. It's not easy to persevere in the face of chronic discouragement. But we have a Savior who has given us the ability to finish the race. Because of Him, we don't have to continue to run with weights hanging on us. When He took our place on the cross, He permanently removed the weight of sin and now encourages us to cross the finish line.

Has life got you down? Discouragement happens to all of us from time to time. When it does, just remember: Never give up, because you're not home yet!

My Inner Garden

Awake, O north wind, and come, O south! Blow upon my garden, that its spices may flow out. Let my beloved come to his garden and eat its pleasant fruits.

SONG OF SOLOMON 4:16

Our backyard flower garden is a lovely place, and we pick and snip it at every opportunity to keep it that way. Beside the lattice that extends to the arbor above, we have planted three climbing vines. Our desire is that the vines will cover the lattice with a beautiful wall of greenery at the end of the patio. But often we have to help the growing tendrils attach to the lattice to grow in the right direction.

One of the other beauties in our garden is a prolific elephant plant—the centerpiece of the primary flowerbed. It seems to grow by inches each day. It grows so fast, in fact, that if left unattended it would overtake the dozens of other colorful plants that surround it and cut off all sunlight from them. Sometimes I think that plant is addicted to Miracle-Gro plant food! So it's necessary to keep it neatly trimmed.

I've noticed that my own soul is like that vine and like that elephant plant. If I don't keep my soul disciplined, I will slip into a soulish—rather than a spiritual—relationship with Christ. Without the discipline of my spirit, my mind would take over and decide in which direction it would focus, and my emotions would choke out some of the good qualities the Holy Spirit

wants to develop in me. I would constantly make will-based decisions rather than receiving heavenly instruction. The *Me* part of
me would block the much needed *Sonlight* that is necessary to
produce the divine beauty in the garden of my heart. Without
spiritual discipline, my soulishness would overwhelm my spirit
where God lives, and I'd become another carnal believer.

The problem with the three climbing vines we planted
beside the lattice is that they seem to have a mind of their own.
They shoot off in every direction except, of course, to climb the
lattice as we intended! Occasionally I must pause to take each
delicate wandering stem and gently thread it through the lattice
to get it to grow in the right direction. If I don't, our beautiful
wall of foliage would have gaps and holes!

Those vines also remind me of my flesh nature. Occasionally
I find myself at rest, sitting quietly in a reflective mode. No problems—all is well. Then I think to myself that this would be an
excellent time to spend with the Lord in prayer and the Word. As
I approach my prayer closet, my mind, my will and my emotions
(my soul) begin to resist in the same way those three vines resist
climbing the lattice. Suddenly I remember phone calls I need to
make, letters I need to write, dry cleaning I need to take or pick
up and dishes I need to wash. What's happening?!

The undisciplined flesh nature in me refuses to cooperate
with what is required to produce spiritual beauty in me. That's
when my inner gardener, my spirit, must step in to provide the
necessary discipline.

The devil is always ready to assist my unruly soulishness. In
fact, he encourages it without invitation. But the Holy Spirit, the
master gardner, stands quietly by to assist my spirit man. Like a
gentleman, He will never force Himself on me. When I encounter
this resistance to intercessory prayer in the inner garden of my
life, I've learned to recognize it immediately. I ask the Master
Gardener for help. Together, we pick, snip and redirect me into

the purposes of God for which I was designed. Then my Beloved, Jesus, can come into His garden and eat His pleasant fruits!

As I close this book, I want you to know that each devotional has come out of my visitation with God in prayer during the last five years. I have given you the framework that will allow you to go beyond the veil and delve more deeply into understanding God's ways for your life.

Now it is your turn. You have been called to a consecrated journey with the Lord. Each day, as you commune with Him, you will make your own divine discoveries and produce your own devotional messages. Out of a consistent and faithful walk with God, your inner garden will flourish and flower with the fruit of His presence in you. Be blessed as you go beyond the veil to learn His ways and walk in His presence.

Fasting

$\mathscr{F}$asting is an often neglected discipline of intercession that carries great potential for spiritual power and answered prayer. Fasting is most often a voluntary abstinence from food to accomplish a specific, God-directed purpose.* As eating strengthens the physical life, so fasting strengthens the spiritual life. When we fast, we are not trying to convince God to do anything, for we cannot control Him.

We must keep a right attitude when fasting. God looks for those who will fast with pure hearts and right motives:

> "Even now," declares the LORD, "return to me with all your heart, with fasting and weeping and mourning." Rend your heart and not your garments. Return to the LORD your God, for he is gracious and compassionate, slow to anger and abounding in love, and he relents from sending calamity (Joel 2:12-13, *NIV*).

Jesus' greatest indictment against the Pharisees was their heart attitude. He said, "And when you pray, do not be like the hypocrites [Pharisees], for they love to pray standing in the synagogues and on the street corners to be seen by men. I tell you the truth, they have received their reward in full" (Matt. 6:5, *NIV*). Later in the same chapter, Jesus repeats:

> When you fast, do not look somber as the hypocrites do,

---

* Note: Use discernment and common sense when beginning a fast. Inform your doctor of your intentions to fast. Do not foolishly and unnecessarily harm your body with an extended fast.

for they disfigure their faces to show men they are fasting.... But when you fast, put oil on your head and wash
your face, so that it will not be obvious to men that you
are fasting, but only to your Father, who is unseen; and
your Father, who sees what is done in secret, will reward
you (Matt. 6:16-18, *NIV*).

The message is clear. God is more impressed with humility
than sacrifice.

The Benefits of Fasting

Spiritual Discernment

There are a number of benefits to fasting; spiritual discernment is one of them. Fasting sharpens our ability to discern
good from evil (see Heb. 5:14). Discernment enhances our ability to see God's perspective in a given situation. Because of her
fasting, Anna, the daughter of Phanuel, saw what others
couldn't. "[Anna] was very old.... She never left the temple but
worshiped night and day, fasting and praying. Coming up to
them [Mary, Joseph and baby Jesus] at that very moment, she
gave thanks to God and spoke about the child to all who were
looking forward to the redemption of Jerusalem" (Luke 2:36-
38, *NIV*). Anna had the discernment, or spiritual insight, to recognize baby Jesus as the promised Messiah after many years of
disciplined fasting.

Increased Ability to Hear God's Voice

Another benefit to the fast is the increased ability to hear
God's voice. Without the direction of the Holy Spirit, intercession is ineffective. It is essential that we discover God's
direction for our prayers. Fasting enhances our ability to

receive divine revelation. The church elders in Antioch agreed to fast and pray for direction regarding Paul and Barnabas. "While they were worshiping the Lord and fasting, the Holy Spirit said, 'Set apart for me Barnabas and Saul for the work to which I have called them' " (Acts 13:2, *NIV*). Just as these elders received direction through fasting and prayer, so can we.

A Christian leader for whom the Lord has called me to intercede is Peter Wagner, who is the chancellor of Wagner Leadership Institute in Colorado Springs, Colorado. On one occasion, Peter's plans were to teach a course on healing to 29 multidenominational Christian leaders at Fuller Seminary in California. These were men and women who minister to the Body of Christ from various nations throughout the world. Although the conference was in California and I was in Texas, the Lord directed me to fast and pray for the needs of these men and women in the class and especially for an outpouring of the Holy Spirit. On the fourth day of my water fast, the Lord spoke to me the name Everett. I felt Him say that He wanted to bring refreshment, encouragement and inner peace to Everett's discouraged heart.

Early Thursday morning, I called Peter. "Peter, do you have a man named Everett in your class?"

"Why, yes," he replied, "there is a man by that name in my class." I shared what the Lord had said. I began praising God that this pastor was to receive the personal touch the Father loves to give His people.

When Peter called out Everett's name in class later that day, he explained the word that God had given me. It was so specific that it even included his name. The young pastor was noticeably touched and received further ministry from others in the class. Peter writes in his book *Prayer Shield:*

> When I got to class, sure enough, Everett Briard, pastor of a Presbyterian Church in Canada, responded with

total astonishment, almost unbelief that such a thing could happen. We as a class prayed for him, and some other pastors ministered to him personally as well. He testified to us that he had felt a definite change in his spiritual and mental outlook.[1]

One week later, this Presbyterian pastor wrote to me, "Dear Alice, your word Thursday morning was the crown and 'clinched' everything for me. I have been overwhelmed by the reassurance that God cares for me and that he would use this way of telling me. Thank you for your part in this. I have a new desire to spend time with God in prayer, and a new love for him. I've been visiting the Prayer Garden at Fuller almost every day."[2]

Nine months later, Peter Wagner wrote in his book:

Everett wrote a letter to me. . . . "I had been struggling with many things for a long time," he said, "not the least of which was the inability to get rid of an underlying sense of meaninglessness, and periodic times of degrees of depression." He said that in a seminar two weeks after the word from Alice he had heard a Christian psychologist say that only through therapy could a person be moved from low self-esteem and self-hate to high self-esteem.

But, Everett said, "God did that for me instantly during your class. He set me free and has given me a sense of newness in ministry. Things which used to throw me into deep despondency no longer have the power to do that. I am so grateful."[3]

Spiritual Power

Spiritual power is another benefit that comes from fasting. Cindy Jacobs writes in her book *Possessing the Gates of the Enemy,*

"Fasting multiplies the effect of prayer at least several times. This is why we often ask for fasting chains along with prayer requests for serious issues. Fasting will touch things that prayer alone will not affect."[4]

As we humble ourselves, the Father gives us the spiritual power to carry out His plan; we shouldn't seek spiritual power as an end to itself. We are to seek the Lord. We are His vessels, and our motives must remain pure if He would empower us for ministry. Luke 4:1-2 says, "Jesus, *full* of the Holy Spirit, returned from the Jordan and was led by the Spirit in the desert, where for forty days he was tempted by the devil. He ate nothing during those days, and at the end of them he was hungry" (*NIV*, emphasis added).

Verse 14 says, "Jesus returned to Galilee *in the power of* the Spirit, and news about him spread through the whole countryside" (*NIV*, emphasis added). We see that Jesus entered the temptation full of the Spirit, but He exited the temptation in the power of the Spirit! From this point in Jesus' ministry, great signs and wonders were performed! I believe fasting was the key.

Increased Faith

Fasting also increases our faith. There are two levels of faith. There is faith *in* God, which leads to our salvation and enables us to receive His blessings. Beyond that, there is the faith *of* God, which empowers our lives. The disciples could not cast out a particular demon in Mark 9:17-19,28-29. Jesus rebuked them for their lack of faith. Then He revealed a key to the Kingdom. Some ministry assignments require more faith than others. They require more than simple faith in God; they require the faith *of* God. For such assignments, fasting with prayer is the answer. Paul learned to live "by the faith of the Son of God" (Gal. 2:20, *KJV*). It is the faith of God at work in us that produces spiritual anointing and authority in the area of deliverance from demons.

Jesus said, "This kind does not go out except by prayer and fasting" (Matt. 17:21).

On one occasion during my prayer time, I asked the Lord about several people with whom I was going to be ministering deliverance. I sensed that these sessions were going to be difficult. As I interceded, the Father spoke gently to my heart and said, "If you will fast for 10 days, I will give you complete victory over these demons." As I sought the Lord's will and not my own, the Lord gave me the grace to start the 10-day juice fast. When I began the ministry time, my faith was literally soaring. I spoke to the demons with divine confidence in the blood of Jesus Christ, and every one of them was defeated!

Increased Focus on the Eternal

Fasting makes us heaven hearted. It increases our perception of the unseen world. Our inability to focus on Christ and His Word is one of the greatest hindrances to our hearing the Lord. Fasting removes distractions that hinder our concentration.

In fact, we can fast from any pleasure, because the issue isn't food but self-denial. The Lord may lead you into a fast from television, sweets or other specific foods or activities. Abstinence from anything that influences our physical senses sharpens our spiritual senses. We can see the Lord and His plans more clearly. Any believer who denies his flesh in an act of humility before the Lord is a threat to the kingdom of darkness!

The Word of God shows us clearly that the battlefield is in the mind:

> The weapons we fight with are not the weapons of the world. On the contrary, they have divine power to demolish strongholds. We demolish arguments and every pretension that sets itself up against the knowledge of God,

and we take captive every thought to make it obedient to Christ (2 Cor. 10:4-5, *NIV*).

A mind transformed by fasting will help us focus on what God is doing in the heavenlies (see Rom. 12:2).

Next, our fasting enables us to see with spiritual eyes. This is the age of the Holy Spirit. He is doing a new thing in the earth. He wants to teach us, equip us and give us new eyes. This includes the distribution of spiritual gifts and manifestations of the Spirit, such as the word of knowledge, word of wisdom, discernment of spirits and faith for a diversity of miracles. Jesus did not exercise any power by Himself but only in obedience to His Father's will (see John 5:19). The Holy Spirit worked through Him to do miracles. Today, we can expect to do the same or greater than Jesus did, because we have access to the same Spirit and there are more of us (see John 14:7). This truth is an area of faith that few of us are experiencing.

"Now faith is being sure of what we hope for and certain of what we do not see" (Heb. 11:1, *NIV*). The Holy Spirit illuminates God's Word. From that illumination, faith rises in our burdened hearts. We trust the Lord to manifest Himself visibly in the earthly dimension what we see in the heavenlies. Fasting has a way of doing just that. It sharpens our spiritual sight. Paul said in 2 Corinthians 4:18 (*NIV*), "So we fix our eyes not on what is seen, but on what is unseen. For what is seen is temporary, but what is unseen is eternal." He was seeing with spiritual eyes (see also 1 Cor. 2:1-12).

As we become single-minded through fasting and prayer, our spiritual vision comes into focus. Often the Holy Spirit tries to call us to Himself, but we are slaves to our flesh. Our faith should rest not on the wisdom of men but in the power of the Spirit. Why? Because God wants us to have spiritual insight. Faith is militantly holding on to that which looks impossible.

I was only 20 years old in 1970, and I yearned to know the ways of God. I did not understand His ways, but I wanted to be an instrument of His grace and mercy. One early morning around two o'clock, as I lay face down on the floor, I asked the Lord to use me in any way that would bring Him pleasure. I surrendered my desire for ministry to Him. I released my possessions, my husband and children. With a broken and sincere heart, I gave Him all I was or ever hoped to be! I would go anywhere and do anything He asked. After pouring out my soul, I asked Him to share with me what might be on His heart for which I could pray.

I will never forget that night, for He revealed several remarkable things to me. I will share with you one of them. God said that Trace, the daughter of a family we knew in California, would be healed. Trace had a lazy eye, and her parents were already planning her eye surgery. With absolute faith, I wrote down these words I had heard and went to bed. It never crossed my mind to analyze if it was God or the devil who was speaking to me. Furthermore, I did not ask whether or not the dispensation of God speaking to man was over! I just believed and received what I had heard. The next day, I called Trace's mom and said, "Carol, I believe the Lord wants to heal Trace of her lazy eye. Just pray for her, believing that the Lord is going to heal her. Please do not schedule the surgery just yet. I am fasting for her healing." Around four weeks later we received a call from California. Just as Jesus had promised me, He healed Trace!

Fasting also enables us to express humility before God. When convicted of sin, we should humble ourselves. In His Word, God gives us some convincing examples of His mercy.

In 1 Kings 21, King Ahab wanted the vineyard that belonged to Naboth. But Naboth was not interested in a deal, and he refused all the King's offers. Jezebel, Ahab's wife, conspired against Naboth. She had Naboth killed because her husband, the king, was having a pity party, sulking over not owning the vineyard himself. After Naboth's death, King Ahab took possession of the vineyard. The word of the Lord came to the prophet Elijah:

> Say to him, "This is what the LORD says: Have you not murdered a man and seized his property?" Then say to him, "This is what the LORD says: In the place where dogs licked up Naboth's blood, dogs will lick up your blood—yes, yours!" When Ahab heard these words, he tore his clothes, put on sackcloth and fasted. He lay in sackcloth and went around meekly. Then the word of the LORD came to Elijah the Tishbite, "Have you noticed how Ahab has humbled himself before me? Because he has humbled himself, I will not bring this disaster in his day, but I will bring it on his house in the days of his son" (vv. 19,27-29, *NIV*).

Although he was perhaps the most wicked king in Israel's history, Ahab found mercy from God through fasting and repentance.

The only fast appointed by Mosaic law was on the Day of Atonement. Leviticus 16 describes the requirements for the high priest in preparation for that day. Moses writes, "This is to be a lasting ordinance for you: On the tenth day of the seventh month you must *deny yourselves* and not do any work—whether native-born or an alien living among you" (v. 29, *NIV*, emphasis added). He repeats, "You must *deny yourselves*; it is a lasting ordinance" (v. 31, *NIV*, emphasis added).

On the Day of Atonement, the high priest and all the people of Israel were to fast for 24 hours. They were not to do any work. They were to humble themselves before God. As the mediator, the high priest would enter the Holy of Holies with the blood sacrifice. He would stand in the gap between the Lord and the sins of the people. As he sprinkled the blood on the mercy seat on behalf of the nation of Israel, their sins were forgiven for another year.

Jesus was the fulfillment of a "better testament" (Heb. 7:22, KJV). The veil of the Temple was torn in two when our spotless Lamb was sacrificed on the cross (see Matt. 27:51). This event gave all who believe in Him free access into the Holy of Holies, the Lord's presence, by the blood of Christ (see Heb. 10:19-22).

A priest was a bridge builder between the people and God. He fasted for the sins and needs of the people. Intercessors, too, are priests, or bridge builders, who go before the throne of God and plead the cause of others. Today we fast and humble ourselves for the sins and needs of people as priests of the Most High God. The incense of our prayers goes before our loving Father.

Fasting is not done out of duty or ritual. The reason for fasting during the Day of Atonement was to appeal to the heart of God on behalf of others. Consider your fast as a love gift to the Lord. Humble yourself and deny your flesh. The Father will see your sacrifice on the altar and will receive it. Your fast is to come from the heart. Your sacrificial gift of fasting on behalf of others will stir the heart of God.

We should also fast when we face impossible situations. Daniel had determined in his heart that the spirit of Babylon would not defile him. Instead of eating the king's food, Daniel ate only vegetables and certain grain breads and water (see Dan. 1).

Later, Daniel was given great authority in the king's palace. The governors and administrators were jealous and wanted to remove Daniel from his influential position. Chapter 6, verse 4 (NIV) says, "They could find no corruption in him, because he was trustworthy and neither corrupt nor negligent." They resorted to trickery and enticed King Darius to issue a decree that anyone who prayed to another god would be thrown into the lion's den. When he was found praying to God three times a day, Daniel was reported to the king. King Darius was saddened, for Daniel was his friend. However, as required by the decree, Daniel was cast into the den of lions. Humanly speaking, this was a situation that was impossible to survive. "Then the king returned to his palace and spent the night without eating and without entertainment being brought to him. And he could not sleep" (Dan. 6:18, *NIV*).

The next morning the king himself went to the lion's den and called out to his friend, "Daniel, servant of the living God, has your God, whom you serve continually, been able to rescue you from the lions?" (v. 20, *NIV*). Daniel answered, "My God sent his angel, and he shut the mouths of the lions. They have not hurt me, because I was found innocent in his sight" (v. 22, *NIV*). I find it intriguing that King Darius fasted from food, from entertainment and from sleep because of Daniel. The Lord then moved the lions to fast from eating Daniel! God honored the sincere fast of King Darius, an unbeliever!

The Bible contains many accounts of believers who fasted to seek God's protection. Ezra led the people to fast and pray in preparation for a safe journey to Jerusalem. Ezra did not want to ask the king's soldiers to protect them because he had told the king, "'The gracious hand of our God is on everyone who looks to him, but his great anger is against all who forsake him.' So we fasted and petitioned our God about this, and he answered our prayer" (Ezra 8:22-23, *NIV*). So with the temple treasures in their care, they fasted for protection and guidance. Four months later, they arrived safely in Jerusalem.

Finally, we also fast to gain victory over powers of darkness. I learned to fast when Eddie and I started working in the area of deliverance. I had never believed in demons until I saw a manifestation of one! Believe me, that will make a believer of the greatest skeptic! After a revival service one evening, a woman came up to Eddie and me and said calmly, "I am demon possessed; can you help me?" The hair on my head stood on end! What were we to do? We could not just say, "Thank you for sharing with us, now have a good day." Occurrences like this catapulted me into warfare prayer and fasting. I am quite sure my motives for fasting were not always pure, but God knows our hearts. Fasting clarifies the mind, purifies the heart and fortifies the spirit. At that time in my life, I was willing to do almost anything for additional anointing!

It is funny to look back on those days. Eddie and I would stay up all night in an attempt to help free some of these people. In Mark 9, a man whose son has a deaf and dumb spirit brings his son to Jesus. After a frustrating failure, the disciples asked the Lord why they could not cast out the spirit. Jesus replied, "This kind can come out by nothing but prayer and fasting" (Mark 9:29). I had remembered the fasting part from this Scripture, but Eddie and I were too busy trying to cast out devils to seek the Lord in prayer. We were exhausting ourselves chasing demons when we should have been chasing after God! Timing, obedience and anointing are crucial in deliverance and spiritual warfare.

Isaiah 58 tells us that a true fast brings deliverance. In Isaiah 58:6, God gives us several reasons why fasting will bring us this victory. As we fast on behalf of others, He will loose the bands, or cords, of wickedness; He will undo the heavy burdens and let them go free. Notice verse 8 (*NIV*): "Then your light will break forth like the dawn, and your healing will quickly appear."

Jesus said, "*When* you fast" (Matt. 6:16, *NIV*, emphasis added), not *if* you fast. He assumes that we will. We should fast until we are victorious over the powers of the evil one. Throughout history, effective intercessors have fasted frequently.

There are several fasts mentioned in Scripture. They include but are not limited to:

- 1-day fast for self-evaluation—Day of Atonement (see Lev. 16:29-31)
- 1-day fast for entering warfare (see Judg. 20:26-28)
- 1-day fast for deliverance (see Ps. 109, especially v. 24)
- 1- to 3-day fast for mercy instead of judgment (see Dan. 9:3-19)
- 3-day fast for healing (see Ps. 35:13; Joel 2:12-27)
- 3-day fast for covering and protection (see Esther 4:15-16)
- 21-day fast for revelation (see Dan. 10:1-19)
- 40-day fast for spiritual power and dominion as "led by the Spirit" (see Matt. 4:1-11)—I suggest you never begin a 40-day fast without clear, explicit direction from the Lord.

Other occasions that call for fasting include periods of national mourning, times when communion with Christ is broken and times of concern for the welfare of others.[5]

Notes

1. C. Peter Wagner, *Prayer Shield* (Ventura, CA: Regal Books, 1992), p. 167.
2. Everett Briard, personal letter to author, February 6, 1991.
3. C. Peter Wagner, *Prayer Shield*, p. 167.
4. Cindy Jacobs, *Possessing the Gates of the Enemy* (Grand Rapids, MI: Chosen Books, 1991), p. 95.
5. Elmer L. Towns, *Fasting for Spiritual Breakthrough* (Ventura, CA: Regal Books, 1996), pp. 225-226.

Recommended Reading

Alves, Elizabeth. *Becoming a Prayer Warrior*. Ventura, CA: Regal Books, 1998.

Bickle, Mike. *Passion for Jesus*. Orlando, FL: Creation House, 1993.

Billheimer, Paul. *Destined for the Throne*. Ft. Washington, PA: Christian Literature, 1975.

Blackaby, Henry. *Experiencing God*. Nashville, TN: Broadman and Holman, 1994.

Eastman, Dick. *Heights of Delight*. Ventura, CA: Regal Books, 2002.

Edwards, Gene. *The Divine Romance*. Wheaton, IL: Tyndale Publishers, 1994.

Grubb, Norman. *Rees Howells: Intercessor*. Ft. Washington, PA: Christian Literature, 1952.

Guyon, Jeanne. *Experiencing the Depths of Jesus Christ*. Jacksonville, FL: SeedSowers Christian Publishing House, 1975.

Haan, Cornell. *The Lighthouse Devotional*. Sisters, OR: Multnomah Publishers, 2000.

Jacobs, Cindy. *Possessing the Gates of the Enemy*. Ventura, CA: Regal Books, 1995.

Moore, Ralph. *Prayer: Dare to Ask*. Ventura, CA: Regal Books, 2002.

Murray, Andrew. *The Ministry of Intercession*. New Kensington, PA: Whitaker House, 2001.

Pitts, Michael. *Don't Curse Your Crisis*. Tulsa, OK: Insight Publishing Group, 2002.

Sheets, Dutch. *Intercessory Prayer*. Ventura, CA: Regal Books, 1996.

Smith, Alice. *Beyond the Veil*. Ventura, CA: Regal Books, 1997.

_____. *Spiritual Housecleaning*. Ventura, CA: Regal Books, 2003.

Smith, Eddie. *Intercessors*. Houston, TX: SpiriTruth Publishing, 2001.

Smith, Eddie and Alice. *The Advocates*. Lake Mary, FL: Charisma House, 2001.

_____. *Drawing Closer to God's Heart*. Lake Mary, FL: Charisma House, 2002.

Sorge, Bob. *Secrets of the Secret Place*. Lee's Summit, MO: Oasis House, 2001.

Tenney, Tommy. *The God Chasers*. Shippensburg, PA: Destiny Image, 1998.

Wagner, Peter. *Prayer Shield*. Ventura, CA: Regal Books, 1992.

Wright, Alan D. *Lover of My Soul*. Sisters, OR: Multnomah Publishers, 1998.

Ministry Contact

Eddie and Alice Smith travel worldwide teaching on various themes related to revival and spiritual awakening. The Smiths teach together as well as individually on topics including prayer, intercession, deliverance, worship, spiritual warfare, spiritual mapping and Christian living.

For information about hosting the Smiths for a conference in your church or city, please check out their website at www.usprayercenter.org. When you click on Invite the Smiths, you will be shown an invitation form to complete and submit online. Or you can send a blank e-mail to request@usprayer center.org. An auto-responder message will e-mail a speaker invitation form to you.

Prayer Resources

You can order Alice and Eddie's other books and materials, as well as resources they recommend, at www.prayerbook store.com.

Free Newsletters

PrayerNet
Alice Smith is senior editor of this free biweekly informative Internet publication. Join thousands worldwide who receive *PrayerNet*. To subscribe, send a blank e-mail message to prayer net-subscribe@usprayercenter.org.

UpLink

Subscribe to Eddie and Alice's free inspiring monthly postal publication *UpLink* (U.S. addresses only) by calling 713-466-4009 or e-mail your name and mailing address to uplink@usprayercenter.org.

Eddie and Alice Smith
U.S. PRAYER CENTER
7710-T Cherry Park Dr., Ste. 224
Houston, TX 77095
Phone: (713) 466-4009
Fax: (713) 466-5633
E-mail: usprayercenter@cs.com
Website: www.usprayercenter.org
Bookstore: www.prayerbookstore.com